HOW TO WRITE a Research Paper

Also included in the How to Write series:

How to Write an Essay
How to Write Poetry
How to Write a Short Story

HOW TO WRITE a Research Paper

SPARK PUBLISHING

Written by Emma Chastain

Spark Publishing
A Division of Barnes & Noble
120 Fifth Avenue
New York, NY 10011
www.sparknotes.com

Please submit all comments and questions or report errors to www.sparknotes.com/errors.

Library of Congress Cataloging-in-Publication Data

Chastain, Emma, 1979-
How to write a research paper / [written by Emma Chastain].
p. cm. — (How to write series)
Includes bibliographical references and index.
ISBN-13: 978-1-4114-2341-1 (alk. paper)
1. Report writing—Handbooks, manuals, etc. 2. Research—Handbooks, manuals, etc. I. Title.
LB2369.C477 2008
808'.02—dc22

2008019325

Printed and bound in Canada

10 9 8 7 6 5 4 3 2

Acknowledgments

I would like to thank Laurie Barnett, editorial director, for her creativity and kindness. I am indebted to Margo Orlando, my editor, for her expertise, hard work, and enthusiasm. Special thanks to my parents, Anne and David Chastain, for their constant support.

Thanks also to Andy Mannle for his contributions to this book.

A Note from SparkNotes

F. Scott Fitzgerald once said, "All good writing is swimming under water and holding your breath." Maybe this is how you feel when you face a blank computer screen: desperate, a bit scared, and unable to breathe. Not to worry. Even world-famous essayists, researchers, fiction writers, and poets feel this way every time they sit down to write. Writing isn't easy, and it takes a lot of work to write well. The good news is that writing is a skill you can *learn*.

That's where the How to Write series comes in. We give you everything you need to know about how to write well, from thinking to planning to writing to revising. More important, we give it to you straight, in a concise, stripped-down style that tells you exactly what to do at every stage of the writing process. You won't find any ethereal, "writerly" advice in this book. Instead of "inspiration," we give you all the steps of the writing process in the smarter, better, faster style you've come to rely on from SparkNotes.

SparkNotes How to Write a Research Paper is your key to writing great prose. We hope it gives you the confidence to write not only your first word, but also your second and third and fourth . . . Your input makes us better. Let us know what you think at www.sparknotes.com/comments.

Contents

Getting Started

You may not have written a research paper before, but you've been doing research your whole life. If you want to buy a new car, choose an apartment, or decide which college to attend, you start by asking questions and gathering information. This is research. You use research often to solve problems and make good decisions.

The word *research* describes both the activity of finding information and the information that is found. A research paper is simply any paper that involves finding out things you didn't know before and presenting that information. The reason you've been assigned to write one is to teach you how to *do* research as an activity and how to *use* research as material. The good news is that writing research papers is a craft you can learn. We're going to show you how to break down this project into manageable steps.

Define the Research Paper

What is a research paper? First, let's look at the *Merriam-Webster's Collegiate Dictionary* definition of *research*, which can be used as both a noun and a verb:

RESEARCH re•search

n Careful or diligent search

v To search or investigate exhaustively

When you research, you search for information—and in a research paper, you use that information to make an argument. Every assignment is different, but in each case, you're asked to combine two distinct activities:

1. Doing research
2. Writing an academic paper

To further understand what a research paper is, it's useful to discuss what it is not.

- **A research paper is NOT a book report.** Book reports require you to read just one book and report on its plot, characters, and themes. Research papers involve reading many books. Rather than simply reporting facts, research papers require you to synthesize the information you find into a thesis.

- **A research paper is NOT an essay.** In an essay, you analyze a topic and come up with a thesis about it. But you don't necessarily do any research at all. Your argument might come purely from your own ideas.

- **A research paper is NOT journalism.** Most journalists attempt to report the facts without bias or a point of view. When you're writing a research paper, you need to take a position—maybe even a controversial one—and back it up by drawing on your research.

Learn the Types

There are many different assignments for which you'll have to write a research paper, and each will require you to approach research differently. There are four main types of research paper:

1. Historical events
2. Current events
3. Text-Based
4. Personal interest

Each type of research paper has its own unique focus, but all research papers present a thesis and use research to defend it.

Historical Events In a historical events paper, you'll research a historical event as broad as the Civil War or as narrow as the riots at Kent State University and come up with an original thesis that analyzes some aspect of the event.

Current Events A current events paper will require you to investigate some aspect of a political situation or social phenomenon, take a stand, and back it up with research. For example, you might research new weaponry used in Iraq or the growing obesity epidemic in America.

Text-Based Whether you're studying psychology, English literature, religion, or another academic topic, a text-based paper will require you to read key texts, research what other scholars have written about those texts, and then come up with your own informed thesis. For example, psychology students might read Freud's *Interpretation of Dreams*, and English literature students might read *The Turn of the Screw*. These students would then read what's been written about these texts and use that information to back up their own thesis.

Personal Interest A personal interest paper requires you to choose a topic that's of personal interest to you—anything from diabetes to dog breeding to Diego Rivera—conduct research on it, and generate a thesis based on what you discover.

Identify the Parts

All research papers, no matter the type or topic, are generally made up of the same ingredients. Master the construction, and you're halfway there:

- **Introduction:** An interesting beginning that captures the reader's attention and lets him or her know what the paper will be about.

- **Thesis:** A well-defined idea that takes an arguable stance. One of the most common difficulties students have is forming a thesis that is specific enough. A thesis can't be an obvious point with which nearly everyone would agree. It must be an argument that some people might *disagree* with. A thesis requires proof, which is what the body of your research paper will provide. The thesis appears in the introduction, usually as the last sentence.

- **Arguments:** Concise, well-orchestrated summaries of different points of view that link together to build a case. These arguments should come from a variety of sources, and all should be properly documented.

- **Counterarguments:** Possible objections to your thesis. A successful research paper anticipates and answers all possible objections. Any issue truly worth discussing will have many sides, and acknowledging and addressing the complexities of an issue is what makes a paper a *research* paper, rather than an opinion piece.

- **Conclusion:** An ending that does more than just summarize and restate your argument. A conclusion should resolve some question, broaden the issue, and deepen the readers' understanding of your thesis.

In a Nutshell We'll explain each of these parts in more detail later. For now, take a look at the following chart to see what the structure of a research paper *looks* like. A research paper is divided into three main parts:

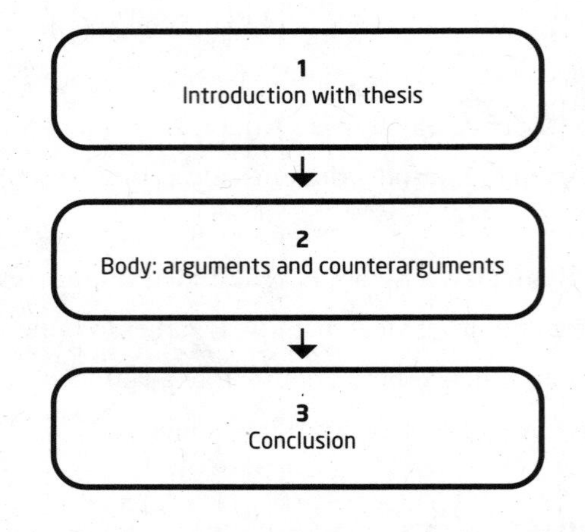

Understand the Grading

Research papers are graded according to four basic criteria. Here they are, in order of importance:

1. Does the paper have a persuasive, convincing argument?
2. Is the argument supported by relevant, careful research?
3. Does the paper showcase analytical thought?
4. Is the paper written well?

You'll notice that the list doesn't mention anything about showing you understand what you learned in class. This shouldn't come as a surprise: a research paper, by its very nature, involves information you find *outside* of class. Notice that the research aspect appears second, not first: if your essay includes a lot of great sources but there's no original, carefully built argument for them to support, your grade will suffer. A research paper isn't just about throwing together a lot of sources; a good paper uses those sources to effectively argue a thesis.

Understand the Process

The process of writing is different for every writer and every piece of writing. Even if you've never thought about it, you probably have your own step-by-step process for writing everything from poems, emails, and blogs to essays and reports. There's a process for writing research papers as well, and understanding it will help you write your paper as efficiently and painlessly as possible. Think of it as a four-phase process:

1. Planning
2. Researching
3. Writing
4. Polishing

Each phase will take a different amount of time, depending on the assignment, type and amount of research, and length of paper. But generally, each phase will always consist of the same steps. Some of these steps are more concrete than others. When you're doing research, for example, you'll actually be walking around in the library stacks, scribbling on notecards, and doing other satisfying physical activities. But when you're creating your thesis, you might make a few jots on your paper or notes on your Word document, but mostly you'll be staring off into space and thinking. No matter how abstract the task, it will be helpful to think of it as another item on your checklist that you must complete before moving on.

Planning Planning your paper carefully will help you create an organized paper efficiently and on schedule. You should do the following:

- Analyze the assignment.
- Make a schedule.
- Brainstorm and generate ideas.

Researching Without research, you won't have a research paper. In this phase, you'll focus on building up the foundation for your arguments. You'll do five things:

- Gather research materials.
- Develop research questions.
- Focus on a topic.
- Form a hypothesis (a working idea for your thesis that you will modify via research).
- Read and take notes on the research materials you have gathered.

Writing All of your work in the planning and researching phases will culminate in a first draft. During the writing phase, you'll do the following:

- Create your thesis.
- Organize your research into a clear outline.
- Write a complete first draft of your paper.

Polishing A first draft will leave room for a lot of improvements, and during the polishing phase, you can make your writing and ideas shine. You'll do three things:

1. Edit
2. Revise and rewrite
3. Touch up and refine

Make a Schedule

A research paper is likely not the only thing on your plate. You have classes, assignments, and exams to deal with too. It might be tempting to wait until the last minute to get started on your research paper, but be forewarned: it will be almost impossible to do a good job because of that pesky *research* requirement. If you get started a night or two ahead of the due date, you'll find yourself frantically Googling for information and fruitlessly attempting to speed-read a teetering stack of books. So make up a reasonable schedule and get an early start.

Giving yourself enough time to research and write has benefits beyond just a good grade:

- **Relaxation:** If you start early, you can work at a consistent pace and avoid burning out. You'll feel relaxed and confident rather than terrified and stressed.

- **Deep Thoughts:** Serious thinking takes time. If you give yourself enough time, you can really delve into the material, think long and hard about your thesis, and write an original paper.

- **New Directions:** As you're reading and collecting material, you might find that your hypothesis has changed completely or that the topic you originally wanted to write about isn't as interesting as another topic you've discovered while doing research. If you've given yourself enough time, you can follow these new directions.

You probably won't start your paper during the first week of the semester or term. But you can keep the paper in mind as you're attending classes and doing homework. As you work, think about the research paper assignment and start considering different topics and questions that interest you. That way, when you sit down to get started, you'll have a few possibilities already in mind.

Scheduling in Action In most cases, you probably won't need more than four weeks to write a five- to ten-page research paper, and you may need much less time. But let's assume you have four weeks to write an eight-page research paper. If you factor in all the other work you have to do, you might decide you can spend about 2 hours each day, or 40 hours total, on your paper. You could draw up the following schedule:

Task	Amount of Time
1. Analyze assignment	½ hour
2. Brainstorm and generate ideas	2 hours
3. Gather research materials	5–7 hours
4. Develop research questions	1 hour
5. Focus on topic	1 hour
6. Form hypothesis	½ hour
7. Read and take notes	6–12 hours
8. Create a thesis	1 hour
9. Organize research	2 hours
10. Write rough draft	4–6 hours
11. Edit	2 hours
12. Revise and rewrite	2–4 hours
13. Polish	1 hour
Total:	maximum 40 hours
	minimum 28 hours

After you figure out how much work you have, look at the due date for your paper. Working backward, you should give yourself deadlines: one for finishing your research, one for writing your rough draft, and one for finishing the final paper. By scheduling carefully, you won't be surprised to find yourself with a paper looming unexpectedly—with no time to do research.

Brainstorming and Choosing a Topic

Choosing a topic might seem less daunting than, say, trolling the stacks for books or figuring out your thesis. After all, choosing a topic is something you can do mostly in your head. It's not as labor-intensive as hunching over your computer, refining your supporting paragraphs, and writing citations into the wee hours.

But it's dangerous to underestimate a great topic's power to lead to an A+ paper—and a *bad* topic's power to doom your paper before you even start writing. Forget about poor writing and a weak thesis. Most research papers are crippled from the start because of a topic that's too broad, too obvious, or just too boring to the writer. Some papers are severely compromised by a topic that's impossible to research adequately. Your topic guides your research and your thesis. It even guides your attitude toward your paper. So if you pick your topic with care, you'll be well on your way to writing a great research paper.

Understand the Assignment

When your instructor assigns a research paper, the assignment may be specific or broad. In some cases, you'll be asked to write on whatever interests you most, with little or no direction. The following are the three most common types of assignments:

1. **The Open-Ended Assignment:** You are allowed to write about whatever topic you choose.
2. **The Choose-One Assignment:** A choice of two, three, or more topics is provided, and you have to decide which one interests you most.
3. **The Predetermined Assignment:** Your instructor has already determined which topic you'll write on, and you have no choice in the matter.

Each of these assignment types has drawbacks and advantages. If you are given a predetermined assignment, you don't have to do as much mental heavy lifting, but you might get stuck with a topic you're not crazy about. If you are given an open-ended assignment, you have more creative control, but you also have to think hard about all of the options open to you. Whatever the assignment, the importance of carefully choosing a topic remains the same.

Spark Your Interest

As you start brainstorming and thinking about your topic, our most useful advice to you is this: You must choose a topic that *interests you*. Maybe you're taking a class about the history of American pop culture and loving every second of it, and your only task when choosing a topic is to decide whether you feel more passionate about Andy Warhol or about the influence of the "I Want *You*" ad. Or maybe you're taking a class on

American literature and spend a lot of time trying to decide whom you hate more, Horatio Alger or James Fenimore Cooper. Either way, it's crucial to choose a topic that you'll really enjoy researching, pondering, and writing about.

Making Connections If you already love your class, choosing a topic for your research paper can be a pleasurable task. But what if you dislike your class? Believe it or not, you can still find a topic you're interested in and maybe even one you feel passionate about. The key is to make connections between the class material and your own interests. For example, suppose you're taking an Intro to Sociology class and are bored to tears by the subject matter. What to do? Pay close attention in class, monitor your own reactions to the reading assignments, and go over your notes until you find some theory or piece of information, no matter how small, that sparks your interest. Maybe you hate Weber and Marx and everything they write. Maybe you hate nearly all of *The Puritan Work Ethic* too, but a discussion about repression is interesting. Pounce on that scrap of interest and use it to find a topic that will keep you engaged.

Avoiding the Easy Out We know how tempting it is to choose your topic based on what seems easiest to research and write about, but don't fall into that trap. No matter how much you try to feign interest, your teacher will sense that you're faking it, and your research paper will be boring and lifeless. But if you choose a topic that actually fascinates you, the process of researching and writing will be much easier to handle. It might actually be kind of fun!

Brainstorm

Making connections between your interests and what you're studying is part of brainstorming, an important step in finding a topic for your paper. When you brainstorm, you let yourself "free think," coming up with lots of ideas without censuring yourself. Later, you'll have to think about whether you'll be able to find enough research on your topic, but for now, just concentrate on generating ideas, even if they seem wacky or overly ambitious. Everyone brainstorms differently: you can make lists, or you might draw connected bubbles with related ideas linked with lines. Don't worry about form. The important thing is to write down whatever comes to mind.

It might seem as if brainstorming is useful only for open-ended essays, but you'll find that it helps even if your instructor has given you a topic or a choice of two or more topics. Here are ways to think about brainstorming for each kind of assignment:

- **Brainstorming for an Open-Ended Assignment:** Consider your own passions and interests, and then brainstorm about how they relate to the class. List everything that you'd enjoy researching and writing about.
- **Brainstorming for a Choose-One Assignment:** Brainstorm ideas about each of the possible topics, taking them one at a time. If you're coming up dry on one or more of the possibilities, eliminate it and focus on brainstorming about the remaining choices.
- **Brainstorming for a Predetermined Assignment:** Write down your ideas and initial impressions about

the assigned topic. Come up with as many thoughts as possible. You'll eventually turn the best of these ideas into your thesis and supporting paragraphs.

Intensifying the Brainstorm If you're lucky or inspired, you'll be bursting with possible topics and ideas. But if you find yourself staring into space and not getting much down on paper, don't worry. There are ways to boost the intensity of your brainstorm:

- **Review:** Look over class notes. Your memory will be jogged, and you might find something interesting your teacher mentioned in passing.
- **Expand:** Check out related websites, message boards, and blogs to see what experts and interested nonexperts are writing about your subject.
- **Talk:** Chat with your classmates about their topic search. Of course you can't steal their ideas, but you can get inspired by what they're planning to research.

Ideas, Not Arguments Brainstorming for a research paper is different from brainstorming for an essay. For an essay, you can make detailed brainstorming charts that contain all your ideas for both possible topics *and* possible arguments, reasons, and examples. An essay relies solely on your own ideas and analysis, so thinking deeply about arguments is an important part of the brainstorming process. A research paper, on the other hand, relies on outside sources, and you often won't know what sort of arguments you want to make until you start reading sources and taking notes.

When you're brainstorming for an open-ended research paper, focus on finding a topic that is, in and of itself, appealing to you. Or, if you've been given a choose-one or predetermined topic, focus on making connections between your own interests and the topic or topics. You'll come up with possible arguments once you start doing research.

Choosing the Best Topic After you've come up with tons of possible topics for an open-ended assignment, you'll have to choose the one topic that will work best. If you're dealing with a choose-one assignment, you'll have to select which topic to write on. If you're dealing with a predetermined topic, you won't have to choose the topic itself, but you'll have to figure out which of the ideas and personal connections you brainstormed will serve as the most useful approach for your paper.

Brainstorming in Action You brainstorm slightly differently for an open-ended assignment than you do a predetermined or choose-one assignment. Take a look at these examples:

Open-Ended Assignment *Write a research paper exploring one element of a film comedy.*

In this case, you have to brainstorm possible topics and ideas without editing yourself or thinking about what kind of research you'll be able to find. You might come up with a list like the following:

Physical humor—Three Stooges, Charlie Chaplin films

Fashion and Diane Keaton in Annie Hall

Annie Hall characters rely on psychology in a funny way

Romantic comedy

Bill Murray's deadpan delivery

Cultural differences in American and foreign films

Humor in French films

Funny females

Cartoons

Choose-One Assignment *Write a research paper about one of the following two topics as it relates to the field of psychology:*

- *Learning*
- *Pain tolerance*

In this case, you have to brainstorm possible ideas for how you'd approach each of the topics. You should try to make connections between the topics and your personal interests to see which topic you're most interested in researching. You might come up with a list similar to the following:

Learning

- *Nature vs. nurture*
- *Cousin is learning disabled—what that means, how he's overcome it, dealt with it*
- *Conditioning*
- *Phobias*
- *The Little Albert experiment*

Pain Tolerance

- Nervous system

- Different cultures experience pain differently

- Cancer victims can often live for years with incredible pain (Aunt Rene)

- Athletes sometimes keep playing even when in pain (remember: finishing basketball game after breaking arm last year)—why is this? Fascinating

- Relationship of patriotism and pain tolerance in soldiers in the Iraq war

Predetermined Assignment *Write a research paper about the social construction of gender.*

In this case, you know what you have to write about, so you need to brainstorm possible ideas for how you'd approach this topic. You need to make connections between the topic and your personal interests—this will help ensure that you write an engaging paper. You might come up with the following type of list:

Social Construction of Gender

- Sex isn't gender

- History of gender

- Biology vs. psychology

- Society finds it funny when gender isn't clear—a cultural joke—such as the "Pat" character on Saturday Night Live

- There are biases about men who don't "act like men"—men who like to cook, paint, shop, or dress well are labeled as "gay"

- Freedom of expression
- The "feminine" man is often mocked on TV—movies and shows that revolve around the question, "Is he gay?"
- American views of what constitutes "masculine" vs. "feminine" are different from other countries' views

Focus Your Topic

To narrow down your options after you brainstorm, you should look for topics or approaches that have the right focus. If your topic or approach is too broad, you'll feel overwhelmed and panicked as you sort through your mountain of research material. If your topic or approach is too narrow, you'll feel annoyed and frustrated that you can't find enough material to use.

Almost all students err on the side of broadness and get overwhelmed. To make sure that your topic or approach is specific enough, you should look for subtopics. A **subtopic** is a topic within a topic. Go through your list of topics or ideas and see if any of them contain subtopics, and list them. For example, for the topic "conditioning," you might list these subtopics:

- Types of conditioning
- Major theories
- Most famous researchers, experiments
- Current scientific and psychological uses

Each of these subtopics is narrow and specific, and you could write a good research paper on any of them. Make sure the topic you choose is as narrow as "current scientific and psychological uses of conditioning" versus the too-broad "conditioning." On the other hand, if you try to write a paper on a very narrow topic such as "the Little Albert experiment," you might not find enough information. You can easily describe the experiment, but there won't be much for you to research, since the experiment is straightforward and not difficult to recount.

Focusing Ideas When you're dealing with a choose-one assignment or predetermined assignment, use this same sort of analysis on the *ideas* you've come up with. For example, for the topic "Social Construction of Gender," we'd be hard-pressed to contain the sprawling "history of gender" in a research paper, while some of the other ideas—particularly, how social constructions of gender work in TV and movies—could make for a great paper. In this way, you can cross out ideas and figure out which topic to choose or which idea or ideas to focus on.

Do Preliminary Research

When writing a research paper, you face the challenge of choosing a topic or approach that you'll be able to research effectively. When it comes time to weed out the topics or approaches you *don't* want to use, do some preliminary research. This means looking around on the internet and taking a quick trip to your library just to see what's out there. There's no need to take notes or read lots of text. The purpose of preliminary research is to get the lay of the land.

Keep these questions in mind as you look:

- Are there plenty of resources—books, articles, reputable websites, journals—on my topic or approach?
- Will I be able to understand the resources available?
- Will I be able to access all of the resources necessary to write my paper?

There are several kinds of topics or approaches that, while interesting, would be difficult to research. Make sure you eliminate from your list anything that is too current, too advanced, or too investigative.

Too Current It's great to draw inspiration from newspapers and magazines, but beware of trying to write a paper on something that's happening as you're conducting research. If you wanted to write about the relationship of patriotism and pain tolerance in soldiers in the Iraq war, for example, you'd have a hard time finding any conclusive or thorough research, even a year or two after the war is over. While you would be able to find plenty of newspaper articles on the apparent effects, you would have trouble finding the kind of scholarly books and articles that research papers require. Those books are themselves the product of careful research, so they take a while to be published.

Too Advanced In class, your instructor may touch on topics that inspire you but that may ultimately be too advanced for your research paper. Suppose your film theory teacher mentions that there are major differences in how humor is portrayed in American and foreign films. You're really interested in this idea and consider researching how French films, in particular, portray humor. This is a good topic, but you should consider how possible it would be for you to research it. If researching your topic will involve addressing cultural works you may not understand, new languages, or unfamiliar jargon, or if you're hard-pressed to understand the key articles other scholars have written on your topic, you'll probably need to choose something more manageable.

Too Investigative While there is a wealth of information available in libraries and online, some information is hard to access. If you want to do research on government secrets surrounding the war in Iraq, for example, you'll have no problem finding ranting blogs and websites of dubious origin, but you'll have a difficult time finding reliable, academic sources. Make sure you're writing a research paper, rather than an *investigative* research paper.

Understand Your Audience

It's important to think about who will be reading your paper and what level they expect your paper to be on. Most students will have their teacher for an audience. Some might be presenting their research paper to a conference or a group of their peers. No matter what audience will be reading your paper, it's important to think about that person, or those people, as you're choosing your topic or approach. You should consider your topic's level and uniqueness when thinking about your audience.

Level You probably have an intuitive sense of the level your audience expects. The key thing here is to not pick a topic or approach that is too easy or unsophisticated in the hopes that your audience won't notice, or that you can jazz up your paper so entertainingly that they won't care. Your teacher will know instantly if you're faking it.

Uniqueness You'll win your audience's heart if you choose a topic that hasn't been done a million times before. For example, suppose your teacher has just read her fiftieth research paper on young love in *Romeo and Juliet*. She turns to your paper, number fifty-one, and finds that it's on the geography of *Othello*. She is delighted before she reads a word, simply because she knows she's going to read about something new. It's most important to write about what interests you, and if that's *Romeo and Juliet*, you'll be able to find something unique and fresh to say. But originality is worth striving for. Even if you've been given a topic, look for a new or surprising angle on it.

Provoke Debate

The topic of your research paper should be one that could inspire a heated debate between you and your friends over dinner. If your topic is one that would make everyone nod, smile, and murmur agreement, it's not appropriate for a research paper.

Your ideal topic will also inspire debate *in you, yourself*. If you begin the research process with an unwavering opinion about your topic, you're going to write a boring, one-sided, totally unconvincing essay. Suppose you want to research Americans' ideas about the death penalty, a punishment you firmly oppose. Even if you try your best to be objective, you're going to gravitate toward authors, journals, and newspapers that share your views. Those will seem logical and well reasoned to you, and sources that take the opposing view will seem loony and not worth reading. The result will be a lopsided opinion piece, not a research paper. It's far better to choose a topic that is fascinating to you but that you don't have passionate, immovable opinions about.

Choosing a Topic in Action Based on the criteria we've discussed for choosing the best topic from your initial brainstorming, we can narrow down the selections on our brainstorming lists. We can do this by adding notes to our possible topics and ideas, then eliminating anything that doesn't make the grade.

Open-Ended Assignment *Write a research paper exploring one element of a film comedy.*

Physical humor–Three Stooges, Charlie Chaplin films—could work; but not very interesting to me

Fashion and Diane Keaton in Annie Hall—love this idea

Annie Hall characters rely on psychology in a funny way—not sure on specifics; but seems really interesting

Romantic comedy—too broad

> Subtopics: History
> Famous works
> Famous actresses in the genre
> Role of sex

~~Bill Murray's deadpan delivery~~—too narrow

Cultural differences in American and
foreign films—hard to research in depth

~~Humor in French films~~—don't know
French; don't know anything about
French films in general

Funny females—too general; not
sure what I'd write about

Cartoons—too broad

> Subtopics: Differences between cartoons
> for adults and children
> Origins
> Types of animation
> Role of cartoons in film history

We're left with just two choices: "Fashion and Diane Keaton in *Annie Hall*" and "*Annie Hall*—characters rely on psychology in a funny way." If this were our assignment, we could choose either of these as our topic—based on whichever one we were most interested in.

Choose-One Assignment *Write a research paper about one of the following two topics as it relates to the field of psychology:*

- *Learning*
- *Pain tolerance*

Learning

~~Nature vs. nurture~~—not debatable; I feel too strongly about nature

Cousin is learning-disabled: what that means, how he's overcome it, dealt with it—could work

~~Conditioning~~

Subtopics: Types of conditioning
Major theories
Most famous researchers, experiments
Current uses

Phobias—could work

The Little Albert experiment—too narrow

Pain Tolerance

~~Nervous system~~—too broad

Different cultures experience pain differently—could work, but maybe difficult to research

~~Cancer victims—can often live for years with incredible pain (Aunt Rene)—too~~ narrow; not enough to discuss

Athletes sometimes keep playing even when in pain (remember: basketball game after breaking arm last year)—why is this? —could work

Relationship of patriotism and pain tolerance in soldiers in the Iraq war—too current

Here, we're left with a couple of ideas under each of our possible topics. Choosing the best one for our research paper now depends simply on deciding what we're most interested in spending time researching and writing about. For "Different cultures experience pain differently," you can see that we noted possible difficulties in researching the idea. If we chose to go with this one, we'd have to be open to the possibility of not being able to find enough sources, and choosing another approach.

Predetermined Assignment *Write a research paper about the social construction of gender.*

Social Construction of Gender

~~Sex isn't gender~~—too narrow; just one part of idea

~~History of gender~~—too broad!

~~Biology vs. psychology~~—could be interesting, but a bit broad; hard to research

Society finds it funny when gender isn't clear—a cultural joke—such as the "Pat" character on Saturday Night Live—possible

There are biases about men who don't "act like men-men who like to cook, paint, shop, or dress well are labeled as "gay"—possible; tie in to TV/movies

~~Freedom of expression~~—not really closely related; and wouldn't inspire debate

The "feminine" man is often mocked on TV-movies and shows that revolve around the question, "Is he gay?"—possible

~~American views of what constitutes "masculine" vs "feminine" are different from other countries~~' views—interesting to me, but maybe not interesting to my audience (all are Americans)

As you can see here, our remaining topics all relate to the idea of how gender is portrayed in the media. We can think about this approach when it's time to do research and create our thesis.

Form a Hypothesis

Before you head to the library or to Google to start researching your topic, you'll need to come up with a tentative angle on your chosen topic—in other words, you need to decide what question or aspect of it you'd like to address. You need to decide what interests you most about it. You're probably worried about generating a thesis, a firm statement of opinion required in all scholarly papers. Not so fast: we're nowhere near the thesis stage yet. We're at the *hypothesis* stage. The hypothesis is like the kinder, gentler father of the thesis. Let's take a look at one of *Merriam-Webster's Collegiate Dictionary* definitions of the word:

> **HYPOTHESIS** hy•poth•e•sis *n*
> A tentative assumption made in order to draw out and test its logical or empirical consequences

Your hypothesis is "a tentative assumption," a general theory that you'd like to investigate. Note the word *tentative*. You should not be wedded to your hypothesis, looking only for information that supports it and discarding anything that contradicts it. On the contrary, you should be open to revising, changing, or even reversing your original hypothesis, depending on where your research takes you.

Your hypothesis should address one aspect of your topic and give you a way to narrow your focus. It should also be something that interests you. You're going to spend a lot of time researching your hypothesis, so try to come up with something that you genuinely want to investigate and read about for hours.

Let's take a look at a few examples:

Class: International Relations
Topic: The Cold War
Hypothesis: The personalities of world leaders, rather than events, caused the end of the Cold War.

Class: Art History
Topic: Japanese art
Hypothesis: Elements of kabuki theater are exaggerated and eroticized in woodcuts.

Class: Intro to Philosophy
Topic: Marx
Hypothesis: Marxism is impossible to put into practice, so its merits as a theory are irrelevant.

Let Us Show You

In this book, we're going to show you an example of a successful research paper. And we're going to show you how it's put together, step-by-step. In the chapters that follow, we'll do research, create a thesis, develop arguments, write the paper, and include quotations and citations. In this chapter, we've worked on choosing an appropriate topic, and the assignment for which we're going to create a paper is this:

Write a four- to five-page research paper exploring one element of a film comedy.

We've narrowed down our list of ideas, and we're going to write our paper on psychology in *Annie Hall*. We know we're interested in the way the main character, Alvy Singer, uses psychological analysis. We've come up with a hypothesis around this idea: that psychological analysis, one of the key focuses of *Annie Hall*, turns out to be useless for Alvy Singer. Now: let's get started!

Gathering Source Materials

At this point, you should have a topic and an idea of what you're going to discuss, as well as a hypothesis (a prediction about what your research will uncover). But you should *not* have a thesis yet. Your thesis, your specific argument about your topic, will be the product of your research. As you research, you might decide that your original hypothesis is correct and can become your thesis. Or you might decide that your hypothesis is *partly* right but needs to be modified—or that it's utterly wrong. Gathering source materials is the first step in this process of analysis. Let your research guide your thinking, rather than force your research to support a predetermined thesis.

Much depends on the sources you find, so understanding exactly how to gather sources is vital to creating an excellent research paper. A ton of information is out there, and the research process can be daunting—but it can also be fun. Think of this part of the writing process as the time to really figure out what fascinates you about your topic.

Know the Types

When you were in elementary school, you probably relied mainly on encyclopedias and dictionaries when you were writing reports. In high school, your teachers expect you to read novels, articles, and books of criticism. In college or graduate school, you might analyze raw data from experiments, work in a language other than English, or discover previously unread texts. All of these different kinds of sources can be divided into three categories:

1. General
2. Primary
3. Secondary

Which category of source you use most will depend a great deal on what kind of assignment you've been given. In many cases, your instructor will have required or recommended one or more primary sources, and your job will be to track down appropriate secondary sources so that you can understand what critics before you have written about that primary source. In other cases, you'll want to focus on other primary sources written around the time of your area of research. Read on for more detailed descriptions about each type of source.

General Sources General sources are reference books, including dictionaries, encyclopedias, almanacs, general histories, and summaries. Here are a few examples of general sources:

- *Chicago Manual of Style*
- *Encyclopedia Britannica*
- *Webster's Collegiate Dictionary*
- *World Almanac*

Primary Sources Primary sources are original works. They include documents, artwork, autobiographies, first-person accounts, essays, letters, interviews, novels, films, plays, poems, short stories, speeches, and TV shows. Here are some examples of primary sources:

- The Declaration of Independence
- *Letters to Sartre* (letters written by Simone de Beauvoir to her lover, Jean-Paul Sartre)
- *The Crucible* by Arthur Miller
- *The Simpsons*
- *Annie Hall*

Secondary Sources Secondary sources are works *about* primary sources and their authors. They include articles, biographies, editorials, essays, and reviews. Secondary sources argue a point or take a stance on a topic, as you will do in your paper. Here are some examples of secondary sources:

- *Zora Neale Hurston: A Storyteller's Life* by Janelle Yates
- *Critical Essays on John Cheever* compiled by R. G. Collins
- *Andrew Marvell Revisited* by Thomas Wheeler
- *The Crucible: Politics, Property and Pretense* by James J. Martine

Search the Library

The library is the place to begin your quest for resources. There, you can search the electronic catalogue, take a look at the stacks to get a physical sense of how much material is out there on your topic, and consult with the reference librarian.

At this stage in the process, don't be hesitant about grabbing whatever looks potentially useful. The idea is to start broadly and then narrow down as you refine your topic. At the library, you'll be able to find the following types of sources:

- Books
- Journal articles
- Newspaper articles
- Reference material
- Government documents
- Online resources

You have to go about finding each of these types of sources in a slightly different way. Don't worry: soon this will all become second nature. In the meantime, always feel free to talk to your reference librarian about how to find sources. He or she is paid to help you do just that!

Books Good old books are still the best resource around. At the library, you can find books on your topic by searching the electronic book catalogue, which lists all the books available at your library. You can search an electronic book catalogue in three ways:

1. By title
2. By author's name
3. By subject

When you're beginning your research, you'll probably want to search by subject. Enter a keyword or two, like "FDA and

RITALIN," and see what kind of list you get. If you're not getting the results you hoped for, try different variations on the word, phrase, or name in the search field. When you spot a source that looks interesting or potentially useful, write down the following information so you can easily find each book in the stacks:

- Book title
- Author's name
- Call number

A **call number** is simply a code assigned to a book that allows it to be shelved in its proper category. Call numbers are made up of letters and numbers. Your library will organize books according to one of two systems, each of which has a slightly different format for its call numbers:

- **Dewey Decimal System:** Used more frequently in high school libraries. Sample call number: 812H373 Q53
- **Library of Congress:** Used more frequently in college libraries. Sample call number: PS3515.E37 F6

Your library will be organized so that it's easy to find a book once you have the call number. The first time around, ask your reference librarian for help. Soon you'll be familiar with the library.

One more note: the electronic book catalogue can actually help you come up with new ideas for searches, which might lead you to more useful books. Searching by subject is the best way to search for books, but what if you're not sure what subjects fall under your general topic? If your library uses the Library of Congress system, you can use **Library of Congress subject headings** for help. When you type in a subject to search, the list of things that pops up will be Library of Congress subject headings. Take a look at the categories: these might suggest subjects you hadn't considered before. They can also show you just how much, or how little, information is out there on a particular subject.

Gathering Books in Action We have our topic and our hypothesis, and we've begun gathering sources. As a reminder, here's the hypothesis we came up with: psychological analysis, one of the key focuses of *Annie Hall*, turns out to be useless for Alvy Singer. This is fairly broad, and we're not sure yet how we're going to narrow it down—but that's what the research process is all about. Our first step at the library is to search the electronic catalogue. We search by subject for "Allen, Woody." Here's a partial list of our results:

Subject	Titles
Allen, Woody	21
Allen, Woody -- Criticism and interpretation	12
Allen, Woody -- Drama -- Video recordings	1
Allen, Woody -- Interviews	3

Allen, Woody -- Interviews -- Sound recordings	1
Allen, Woody -- Miscellanea	1
Allen, Woody -- Motion pictures	1
Allen, Woody -- Pictorial works	1
Allen, Young John, 1836–1907	1
Allenby, Edmund Henry Hynman Allenby, 1st Viscount, 1861–1936	2

When you do a subject search, you'll get a list of Library of Congress subject headings. Looking at these headings can give you a sense of what's out there and of the different directions your research could take. The first two headings turn up lots of interesting results. We write down the call numbers so we can find the books in the stacks. "Drama -- Video recordings" turns out to be a documentary about Allen's jazz band, which isn't related to our topic. Both of the "Interviews" headings yield potentially useful results. "Miscellanea" is a quiz book, which isn't appropriate for a research paper. "Motion pictures" is an interview with Allen. "Pictorial works" turns out to be a book of photos and essays, which we decide to check out. The last two results are obviously not related to our subject.

As you begin the research process, you'll find that your search results turn up lots of unusable junk. Try not to get too frustrated. As you narrow down your hypothesis and do some preliminary reading, you'll get a better handle on your topic, what interests you most, and what kind of material is available.

Journal Articles At the library, you'll be able find journal articles by searching databases such as *ProQuest*. These databases will show you a small summary of each article—which is really useful as you're doing research—followed by the article in full. Print out any articles you think might be useful. If you don't want to or can't print them out, jot down the following information so you can find the article again later if you want to look at it more closely:

- Title of the article
- Author's name
- Keyword search that brought you to the article

Some of the most popular databases for articles include the following:

- **ProQuest:** A collection of academic journals from a variety of fields, including general interest, business, health, economics, and management.
- **JStor:** An exhaustive online collection of academic journals. JStor covers several areas of study: Arts and Sciences, General Science, Business, Language and Literature, Math and Statistics, Music, Biological Sciences, and Ecology and Botany. Your library may choose to subscribe to all of these collections or only selected ones.
- **Project Muse:** A collection of over two hundred scholarly journals. Most of Project Muse's journals concern the humanities.

- **ScienceDirect:** A collection of journals covering all areas of medicine, technology, and science. ScienceDirect also has a College Edition tailored to college students.

Sometimes the full-text article won't be available online. Don't panic! Most major university libraries have tons of "bound periodicals"—that is, years and years' worth of back issues of major journals bound together in book form. Usually, four or five issues will be bound together in one "book." These have call numbers just like books do. Be sure to note the issue number, issue date, and page number, if available, so you can find the right issue within the bound group. To see whether your library has that particular journal, type the name into the electronic book catalogue search field, or ask your reference librarian.

Great, you might be thinking. *Now I can read all those copies of* Sports Illustrated *and* Mademoiselle! Not so fast. When we say "journals" or "articles," we're talking about the scholarly variety. Scholarly journals are excellent resources, and one of the reasons they're excellent is that each article goes through a rigorous review process before it's accepted and published. Most scholarly journals are **peer-reviewed**, which means that members of a particular academic community must review and evaluate every article to make sure its information is accurate, relevant, and significant.

Newspaper Articles Searching for newspaper articles has changed a great deal over the years. If you were a student ten years ago, you'd probably have to look at old newspaper articles on **microfilm**—that is, very small photographic reproductions of articles that you can see only by viewing those reproductions on a special machine. Now, most major newspapers have put past issues online. How far back you can go depends on the newspaper, but some papers, such as the *New York Times*, have their entire publication history—dating back to the 1800s—available electronically. To find newspaper articles, try searching the following databases at your library:

- **Lexis Nexis:** A collection of articles and journals from general news, law, business, and public records.
- **ProQuest Historical:** An archive of full-text articles from newspapers including the *New York Times*, the *Boston Globe*, the *Wall Street Journal*, and many others.
- **Factiva:** A collection of over 9,000 sources on business and business news.

Reference Material If you need to consult an encyclopedia or a dictionary as you do your research, the easiest method is to use your library's CD-ROM collection. The famous *Oxford English Dictionary* is available on CD-ROM, as are various encyclopedias. Many of these references are also available online—but often for a fee, so it makes sense to utilize your library, which has subscriptions that can be used by anyone.

CD-ROMS, like websites, are searchable, which can make doing research much easier. By pressing CTRL + F, you can search for keywords in whatever document or reference CD-ROM you're looking at.

Government Documents If you're writing a paper on law, Congress, the economy, or any other topic related to the government, you'll be able to access a great deal of information at the library. *GPO on Silverplatter* will allow you to search for government documents. (You can also check online at GPOAccess.com, or in Google's Government Documents database.)

Online Resources Libraries' websites, which bridge the gap between the internet and physical libraries, offer an enormous number of resources. Most of these library websites are available only to subscribers or to students at that particular library's university, and in most cases, you have to actually be in the library to access them. For example, anyone can use the resources on nypl.org, the New York Public Library's website, but to access most of them, you must be in the library itself, using a library computer.

Besides the databases for journal and newspaper articles we've already described, your own library will have some or all of the following online resources available through its website:

- **NetLibrary:** A library of over 100,000 print books available for online download
- **Early English Books Online:** A collection of 96,000 books printed between 1475 and 1700
- Dictionaries
- Encyclopedias
- **ARTstor:** An online museum comprising hundreds of thousands of digitized images

- Other image databases such as the **American Memory Project** and the **AP Photo Archive**
- Indexes of resources on particular topics, such as indexes showing you where to find resources on Gay and Lesbian Studies, Modern American History, Elections, Christianity, and African Studies
- Periodicals

Search Online

Next to the library, the internet will be your most valuable resource as you do research for your paper. You've probably had lots of experience online, doing everything from blogging to updating your MySpace profile. You're most likely an expert searcher who can find the website you're looking for in milliseconds. However, keep in mind that locating academic sources online isn't as instantaneous a process as, say, finding Maureen Dowd's last column in the *New York Times*. You're probably looking for information on a topic that's relatively new to you, and you're going to have to wade through a lot of biased or unscholarly information. So be patient with yourself and leave more time than you think you need.

Starting with a General Search To get a general sense of what's out there, start by doing a search. We recommend Google as the most useful search engine. Still, no matter how good the search engine, you'll have to search carefully in order to find material you can use—and to avoid spending hours sifting through junk. Suppose you're writing a research paper on Spain. If you go to www.google.com and search for *Spain*, you get results on everything from travel to flamenco to Spanish omelets. Try the following search tips:

- If you want to search for a specific phrase, put it in quotes: "Franciso Franco" (This way you'll avoid all the articles and websites about Franco Mirabelli design, James Franco, etc.)

- If you want to find multiple subjects, type *and* between each one: Spain and Franco and poverty

- If a certain word must appear, type + in front of it. If a certain word must *not* appear, type – or *not* in front of it:
  Franciso + Franco – vacation
  or
  Franciso + Franco not vacation.

Using Directories Some search engines allow you to search by directory, narrowing your topic down step-by-step until you have a list of all the relevant articles, websites, images, and so on. For example, go to www.google.com and click on *more*, and then *directories*. If you're writing a paper on child psychology, you would go to *science*, then to *psychology*, then to *child psychology*. From the *psychology* level, you might also go to *journals and publications*, or *people*, or *research methods*. Alternatively, you can click on Google Scholar to search scholarly publications.

Finding Magazines, Journals, and Newspapers

Nearly all major publications have searchable websites. Check out www.nytimes.com, www.wsj.com, www.usatoday.com, www.newsweek.com, and www.timemagazine.com as you're doing research. You may find, however, that the internal search engines these websites use aren't always up to par. If you get frustrated, head back to Google, put "new york times" or whatever source you need in quotes, and add the keyword or phrase you're looking for. This will tell Google to search for entries containing the source name and the word or phrase you need.

Choose Reliable Sources

No matter where you're looking for sources, you should always pay close attention to how reliable potential sources are. You may think that books are always reliable—but do you always believe everything you read? Of course not. Just because something has been published doesn't mean it's reliable. Learning how to evaluate potential sources from both the library and the internet will help you find great sources that can help—not hurt—your paper.

Reliable Books In general, the most useful books will come from academic or governmental sources. Less helpful will be corporate or private publications, since they may have an agenda or bias they're trying to promote. Here is a checklist to help you determine whether or not the sources you've gathered are reliable:

- **The author is an expert in his or her field.** Check out the biography on the book jacket or search the library catalogue to get a list of other books he or she has written.

- **The publishing house is academic.** University presses, such as the Oxford University Press and the University of Chicago Press, publish reliable books. You don't need to rely exclusively on books published by university presses, however—see next item.

- **The book was published fairly recently or is considered a classic.** You can always count on Aristotle and Tolstoy, even though they wrote a long time ago. But be careful when you're looking for books *about* Aristotle and Tolstoy. When it comes to books of this kind, more recent publications will be most useful for you, since they take into account all the latest theories and developments.

Reliable Internet Sources As you know, the internet is full of unreliable information. Be careful to investigate the dependability of the sources you find online. As with books, the best online sources will be academic or governmental. Here is a checklist to help you determine whether or not the sources you've gathered are reliable:

- **The website has one of the following URLs:**
  Educational institution: www.......edu
  Government website: www.......gov
  Corporate/commercial website: www.......com

Non-profit website: www.......org
Military website: www.......mil

- **The author of the article, essay, etc. you're reading is identified and has academic or other relevant credentials.**

- **The website is not a blog or a homepage.**

- **The website is frequently updated.**

- **The website's links work.**

- **The website is not a delivery device for wildly flashing banners and hundreds of pop-ups.**

Look Beyond Stacks and Websites

When you're gathering source materials, don't feel confined to books and online resources. If you want to branch out, feel free to investigate less traditional sources as well:

- Films, documentary and nondocumentary
- Interviews
- Maps
- Photographs
- Questionnaires

When you balance less traditional sources of information with more traditional books and articles, you can create a paper that demonstrates your commitment to seeing the whole picture.

Document

As you print out articles from websites and gather books, it's important to document your sources. It might seem easy to skim and jot down a few notes now, then come back and write down the source info later, but don't risk it. Faced with a huge pile of sources, you'll forget which ones were useful and which note was about which source, and then you'll run the risk of plagiarism. (For more on the issue of plagiarism, see page 68). As you gather sources, make sure you note the key information about each source. You may even want to record this key information in the appropriate documentation style.

Key Information As you collect sources, write down the following information:

- Author's name
- Title
- Publication place
- Publication date
- Page(s) with pertinent information
- URL

This way, you'll know exactly which source is which, and you won't have to do any guesswork when it comes time to choose sources for your paper and, ultimately, document them.

Documenting in MLA/APA Style You might consider documenting your information exactly as it will appear on your works cited or references page. For example, you might write down:

> Pearce, Fred. *Deep Jungle*. Cornwall, England: Eden Project Books, 2005.

This is MLA style for citing books on a works cited page. Documenting info like this is slightly more work now, but it will save a lot of time later. (See Chapter 9, "Citing Sources," for specific details on how to document sources in MLA and APA style.)

Using Source Materials

4

You've gone to the library, combed through electronic catalogues, and printed out lots of articles from the internet. Now you're ready to start using the source materials you've gathered. Your instincts may be to dig in, read with close attention, and take detailed notes. Not so fast! There's plenty of time for that kind of hard work, but the first step is to get an overview of all the sources you've collected and then skim the most promising ones. After you've gotten a sense of the sources you'll be working with, the note-taking can begin.

You may feel daunted by the volume of materials you've gathered, but don't panic. You won't have to read everything, and if you leave yourself plenty of time, skimming, reading, and taking notes can be the most rewarding part of writing a research paper. Now's your chance to explore your own hypothesis, do some hard thinking, and possibly let your research take you in new directions.

Get an Overview

Doing research isn't like reading books you've been assigned for class: *you don't have to read each source from cover to cover.* In fact, you'll find that some sources have just one or two useful paragraphs. You *will* read each word of the most relevant and useful sources, but some sources will require only *skimming*. As you embark on your research, get an overview of each source before you dive in and start reading. The task is to form an impression of each source and judge how useful that source will be. Get the lay of the land by doing the following:

- **Read the jacket flaps and the back cover.** The back cover and jacket flap often provide a short summary of the book, along with quotations and endorsements from experts in the field.

- **Look at the table of contents.** Check to see whether the chapter titles seem relevant to your topic and which ones look especially useful.

- **Read a few paragraphs from different chapters.** Get a sense of the writing style of each source's author. If you're looking at articles, read the opening and the closing paragraphs.

- **Check out the bibliography.** See what sources the author has consulted and how thorough he or she has been.

Sorting Sources As you get an overview of your sources, sort them into two piles: the useful and the not-useful. You might decide later that you've put certain sources into the wrong stack. A book you originally thought looked terrible might turn out to be great, and vice versa. That's fine: these piles are just temporary ways of organizing your sources. Use the following guidelines to help yourself sort.

Useful Sources will be:

- Closely related to your topic
- Endorsed by enthusiastic and well-known experts
- Full of appropriate chapters
- Neither too broad nor too narrow
- Written in a straightforward, clear, prose style

Not-Useful Sources will be:

- Tangentially related to your topic
- Endorsed by professors from disreputable universities
- Either too narrow or too broad
- Written in an overly simplistic or overly complicated prose style

Start Skimming

Before you start reading carefully and taking notes, skim each source in your "useful" stack to get a sense of where the most important information lies. This might take only ten to fifteen minutes per source, and you probably won't need to write down anything as you're skimming. Your goal is to get a better idea of what sources will be the most useful.

Skimming might seem like a waste of time—why not plunge in and start taking notes? But don't skip the skimming step. If you force yourself to get a sense of each source before you pull out those note cards or that laptop, you'll get a better understanding of your topic, and you'll avoid taking notes on less-useful parts of your sources. Skimming saves lots of time in the end. Here's how to go about it:

- **Read the first and last paragraph of each chapter.** Get a sense of the premise and conclusion of each chapter. If you're looking at an article, read the opening and closing paragraphs.

- **Read the topic sentence of each paragraph.** Often, writers use the first sentences of paragraphs—the topic sentences—to set out the specific point they're going to argue. The rest of the paragraph backs up that point or provides evidence. By reading just the topic sentences, you can get an outline of the writer's overall argument in each chapter.

- **Mark information you want to read more carefully.** Instead of slowing yourself down by taking notes at the skimming stage, put a sticky note next to paragraphs you know you want to return to and read more carefully.

Once you're done skimming, you'll not only have a stack of potentially useful sources—you'll also know exactly which of those sources might yield the most promising leads.

Read and Take Notes

With skimming complete, it's time to read and take notes. This is the most intensive and time-consuming part of the research process—and also the most integral part of creating your research paper. Reading your sources and taking notes are the steps that form the foundation for your paper. Once you start writing, you'll be relying heavily on your newfound knowledge and your careful notes. When you read and take notes, you'll be doing six things:

1. Investigating the basic facts about your topic
2. Figuring out the various arguments made by the authors of your sources
3. Finding evidence that supports and refutes your hypothesis
4. Coming up with new ideas of your own
5. Gathering quotations that might be useful in your paper

And, last but not least . . .

6. You're *always* writing down information about the source so that you can cite it on your works cited or references page and find the source again yourself.

You'll learn more about how to read sources skillfully and take great notes in the sections that follow.

Choosing a Format Note cards are the classic note-taking tool, but some students feel more comfortable taking notes on their computers. Each method has its advantages and disadvantages.

If you use note cards, you can write in colored pens, choosing a different color for each kind of note. You can also affix colored sticky notes to your note cards to stay organized. When it comes time to write, you can physically arrange and rearrange your note cards, even spreading your cards on your bed or floor so that you can see the different pieces of what will become your thesis and argument. However, writing by hand can be slow. Also, you'll have to copy quotations and paraphrased arguments into your computer at some point, which can seem like a tedious way to spend your time.

If you use your computer, you can speed up the note-taking process greatly, since you may be able to type faster than you can write. Once you've taken notes, you can use the "Find" feature to quickly access different subjects and keywords, and you can even take notes on an Excel spreadsheet so that you can rearrange information by column. You can also cut and paste quotations from electronic sources rather than retyping them. One problem with this is that you greatly increase the risk of plagiarism. When you're taking electronic notes, it's very easy to copy and paste information from electronic sources and websites—and forget to cite your source. You also won't be able to look at all of your notes at once, and you won't be able to handle your notes physically, rearranging them in your hands.

We suggest using note cards as you read and take notes. If you prefer using your computer, just be sure to monitor yourself and rigorously note your sources.

Stay Organized

You *do not* have to write in full sentences as you're taking notes. In fact, it's much more time-effective to skimp on pronouns and conjunctions and to write down only the essential info. However, you *do* have to take the time to stay organized. The more organized you are while taking notes, the easier it will be to sort through your notes while you're writing your paper. Each note should include the following information:

1. **Subject of the note:** We suggest using the categories Basic Fact, Summary, Paraphrase, Evidence, Counterargument, My Idea, and Quotation.
2. **Note itself:** Make sure you write only one note per card.
3. **Source info:** For a book or online source, include the abbreviated title, author's last name, and page number/website address. For an article, include the journal name, issue date, author's last name, and page number.

Understanding the different subject categories will help you stay organized and avoid plagiarism. Let's take a brief look at each one.

Basic Fact As its name suggests, a Basic Fact note card keeps track of the basics: the dates, definitions, places, people, and so on that you think you'll need at hand as you're writing your paper. For example, suppose you're writing a paper on society's view of stay-at-home mothers, and you're taking notes on Cheryl Mendelson's book *Home Comforts*. A Basic Fact note card might contain the following note:

> *Basic Fact*
> *Mendelson lived in Appalachian Pennsylvania until she was 13.*

Summary Summary notes sum up paragraphs, chapters, articles, or books. They will be useful ways to remind yourself of authors' big ideas, theses, and overarching themes. A Summary notecard for *Home Comforts* might read:

> Summary
> Chapter 59 covers emergency preparedness, incl. medicine cabinets, safe and unsafe products, etc.

Paraphrase Paraphrasing in your paper will be useful when you want to keep writing in your own voice or when the author's words aren't particularly lyrical and therefore aren't worth quoting. Paraphrased notes must do the following:

- Stay true to the author's meaning
- Keep to the general length of the original passage
- Not use any of the author's exact phrasings (unless you want to put those phrasings in quotation marks)

As always, write down the page number where your paraphrased passage occurs. Don't forget: it's plagiarism to paraphrase an author without citation, even if you're not using direct quotations. A paraphrased paragraph from *Home Comforts* might be the following:

Paraphrase
1940s women had to understand only six fibers; 1960s women had to understand double that amount b/c of acrylics, poly., etc. Modern women have to understand 100s more.

Evidence As you read and take notes, you are figuring out how each source confirms, contradicts, or alters your hypothesis. When you come across information that bolsters your hypothesis, make a note of it. (These notes might be paraphrases, summaries, or quotations.) If your hypothesis is that society views stay-at-home mothers as anachronistic relics from the 1950s, a note from *Home Comforts* might be:

Evidence
Mendelson says she felt guilty about liking housekeeping. She tried academia but in the end returned to domesticity because it was her "true nature."

Counterargument It's crucial to remember that doing research is not just a way to prove your hypothesis. As you read, you might decide that your original idea is completely wrongheaded. Even if you stick with your original idea, you'll need to address the arguments against it—the counter arguments. So be sure to note evidence against your topic. (Again, these notes might be paraphrases, summaries, or quotations.) A Counterargument note card might read as follows:

> *Counterargument*
> *Mendelson says there's not much difference between the 1950s and the 1990s: "Although homes in 1955 were startlingly different from those of 1915, they would turn out to be remarkably similar to homes in 1995."*

New Idea Ideally, your sources will ignite all kinds of sparks, and you'll have tons of new ideas as you read. New Idea note cards capture the material that comes from your own head, rather than anything you're reading. For example:

> *New Idea*
> *The more I read this book, the more I think maybe society sees women as generals of the home, esp. in the post-9/11 world. See Chapter 59 especially.*

Quotation When you come across a line that is colorful, unusual, precise, and exactly relevant to your hypothesis, write it down for possible use in your paper. Quotations must be written down exactly as they appear in the source. You should follow the following guidelines:

- If you omit a phrase, use three periods (an ellipses) in its place.
- If you omit a whole sentence or sentences, use *four* periods in their place.
- If you change a capital letter to a lowercase letter, or vice versa, put a bracket around it.
- If you add a word or change the tense of a word, put a bracket around it.
- Put only the original punctuation inside the quotation marks.

Suppose you're writing down part of the following original quotation from *Home Comforts*:

> "Few laws protect domestic employees on the job, but those few deserve our scrupulous observance. Domestic employees–cooks, maids, cleaners, baby-sitters, nannies, housekeepers, gardeners, and drivers–are those who do work in the home that would otherwise be done by members of the household. In people's private houses, such employees typically experience low pay with no health benefits, no pension plans, no vacation pay, no job security, no hope of advancement, and no redress for grievances and injustices except to leave a job they may desperately need."

Your Quotation note card might look like this:

> *Quotation*
> *Mendelson writes, "Few laws protect domestic employees on the job, but those few deserve our scrupulous observance. Domestic employees ... are those who do work in the home that would otherwise be done by members of the household . . .*
> *[S]uch employees typically experience" myriad problems, and have "no redress for grievances and injustices except to leave a job they may desperately need."*

Taking Notes in Action As we research, we're checking out everything from Woody Allen biographies to scholarly works on Freud. Here are some examples of what our notes look like:

> *Basic Fact*
> *Woody's given name: Allan Stewart Konisberg*
> *—Lax p. 9*

Paraphrase
Prof. Kramer says in the 1970s, his med school taught child development from a Freudian perspective.
—Kramer p. 197

Evidence
In Annie Hall, Woody's "in every scene, almost every frame, parading his insecurities, phobias, and deep self-deprecation."
—Meade p. 112

Counterargument
Woody "complained incessantly about analysis," but it was "a definite lifestyle for him."
—Kramer p. 100

My Idea
Interesting that in the movie, Annie Hall gets so much out of analysis, whereas it's useless for Woody's character. Was this the norm for 1970s women?

These notes are all over the place, but that's the way they should be. Don't forget: we're working with a hypothesis that could change as we continue doing research. As long as we stay organized during the note-taking process, we'll be able to go back and shuffle our notes into order during the writing process.

Strike the Right Balance

One of the most challenging aspects of taking notes is to be thorough without getting too detailed. You don't want to start out taking extremely detailed notes, only to run out of time and find yourself forced to abandon what you were reading. On the other hand, you don't want to take such vague notes that later you can't remember what you found important about that particular paragraph or quotation. Let's take a look at a few examples:

- **Too Specific:**

Basic Fact
Editor writes, "More's beginnings were auspicious. The son of Agnes and John More, a barrister, he was sent to be a page in the household of Thomas Morton, Archbishop of Canterbury and Lord Chancellor, and then to Oxford, where he met John Colet (1467?-1519) who became, in More's words, "the director of my life."

There's no need to write down a long quotation of this type because it deals strictly with biographical facts as opposed to an author's opinion. It's a waste of time to copy out each word rather than jotting down just the salient facts.

- **Too Vague:**

> *Basic Fact*
> *More childhood—barrister and page. Religious background. Director of his life.*

While you're taking notes on the paragraph on Thomas More's childhood, you might feel sure that these sparse words will be enough to jog your memory. But chances are you'll be puzzled when you're going over your notes a few days or weeks later and come to something like this. It's just too vague. Who was the barrister and who was the page? What does "religious background" mean? Who was the director of More's life? You'll have to waste time by returning to the source and trying to figure out what your own notes meant.

- **Just Right:**

> *Basic Fact*
> *More's dad was a barrister. Religious job: worked as page for Archbishop. Went to Oxford, where met Colet, "director of my life."*

These notes don't waste time with lots of wordiness or conjunctions like *and* or *but*. They're not written in complete sentences. But they do get the crucial information across so you'll be able to refer to them later and really get the gist of the idea.

Spreading the Love Finding a book or article that you love can be an exciting experience. You might think, "This is great! This writer is saying exactly what I think! I've found the perfect source." No matter how much you admire one book or article, however, be careful not to fall in love. The danger is that you'll accept all of the author's arguments without question and fail to compare them against other opinions or theories. Leaning too heavily on one source will make your paper imbalanced.

Spreading the love is also crucial because this is *your* research paper, and you must make your own original argument. Rehashing someone else's wonderful thesis, or recasting it in a slightly different light, will make your paper a failure.

Avoid Plagiarism

As you read and take notes, it's crucial to know what plagiarism is and how to avoid it. Not sure exactly what it means to *plagiarize*? Take a look at how *Merriam-Webster's Collegiate Dictionary* defines it:

> **PLAGIARIZE** pla•gia•rize *v*
> To steal and pass off (the ideas and words of another) as one's own; use (another's production) without crediting the source

Take a look at your school's academic code and familiarize yourself with its specific definition of plagiarism and the penalties it carries. Most schools take plagiarism very seriously. In the worst cases, expulsion is the punishment for plagiarism, so make sure you avoid it rigorously.

Here are some common forms of plagiarism:

- Passing off another student's work as your own
- Using an author's phrases, sentences, or paragraphs without citing the source
- Paraphrasing an author's ideas without citing the source
- Summarizing a chapter or book without citing the source

Many students know that copying out text without citing it is unacceptable. But some don't realize that even if you're not quoting directly, but instead are paraphrasing or summarizing, *it is plagiarism* unless you cite the source.

Keeping Track of Your Sources You might be thinking, "Of course I'm not going to copy an author's writing." But be careful: it's easy to slip up as you're taking notes. Don't let yourself write summaries, copy out quotations, or cut and paste information from websites without noting the key information about the source. It's tempting to take notes thinking you'll go back later to write down the source info, but there's a good chance you'll forget where you found the information—or that you'll forget that the information came from a book or a website at all and mistakenly think you came up with it yourself. It might sound implausible, but when you're dealing with stacks of books and articles, it's really easy to get confused.

That said, you certainly don't need to write down *all* of the source info you'll need for your works cited or references page on each of your note cards. That would be a waste of time. The abbreviated title, author's last name, and page number will do just fine. As long as you can easily find the source again, you've done your job.

Revise Your Hypothesis

As you read and take notes, you might find that your original hypothesis is getting weaker and weaker. Or you might find that it's really boring in comparison to another idea that popped into your head as you were reading. This is fine—in fact, it's great. The goal of research is to explore, not to prove a predetermined point. Once you've gathered sources and taken notes, feel free to revise your hypothesis to reflect your new or better idea, or jot down some notes about what you've found to be weak or strong about your original hypothesis. Remember: you're not *obligated* to change your hypothesis radically. If your original idea holds water, that's great. But allow yourself to stay flexible and to roll with the punches. Your thoughts about your hypothesis will be important when you start creating your thesis.

Creating a Thesis

When you write a research paper, your job is not only to find information and report on it but also to announce your own take on that information. You're not a slave to the information you've gathered—your research should work for *you*. Depending on the way you use your evidence, you can come up with dozens of interpretations of the same set of facts. You could probably stick with your original hypothesis and back it up using your sources. But it might also be possible to reverse your hypothesis and back *that* up by using those same sources. Your sources are important, but your opinion about those sources—your thesis—is even more so.

It's your responsibility to be faithful to what you've discovered as you did your research. You should never twist the truth just to sound original. But as an interpreter and presenter of the facts, you have a great deal of power. If you come up with a knockout thesis, you can wield that power effectively and persuade your readers to interpret the facts as you do.

5

Define *Thesis*

Take a look at the definition of a *thesis* from *Merriam-Webster's Collegiate Dictionary*:

THESIS the•sis *n*

A position or proposition that a person (as a candidate for scholastic honors) advances and offers to maintain by argument

Let's translate. A thesis is a clear, concise, and unambiguous declaration of what your opinion is on the topic you're discussing. In other words, a thesis isn't the topic itself; a thesis is your *opinion* on the topic. If your paper is about book banning (your topic), your thesis is your *opinion* on book banning—for example, that book banning often increases readers' interest in a book. Your paper will argue that point.

Keep in mind that the key word here is *opinion*. A thesis isn't a summary of the research you've done or a statement of fact about that research. Rather, a thesis presents a *point of view* about what you've read. Your paper will then back up that point of view by presenting evidence and considering counterarguments. While your thesis must be opinionated, it does *not* need to present a black-or-white opinion. You can write a strong thesis that admits the existence of gray areas. For instance, you might argue that your research suggests that the FDA's food pyramid is misleading and dangerous *with exceptions* (for people of a certain age, height, and build, the pyramid's recommendations are accurate).

Requirements for a Successful Thesis A successful research paper thesis is several things. It must be:

1. A statement of opinion
2. Reliant on research

3. Clear and explicit
4. Succinct as possible (no more than three sentences and usually just one)
5. Presented early in the paper (no more than 10 percent of the way in)

No matter what the topic of your research paper is, your thesis must meet all five of these requirements. For the fifth requirement, it's easy to figure out what constitutes 10 percent. If you're writing a two-page paper, your thesis should appear close to the beginning of the first page. If you're writing a five-page paper, your thesis should appear no later than half a page in. And so on. Just remember that the bulk of your paper should be the argument that proves that your thesis makes sense.

Orienting Your Readers The opening paragraph of your paper prepares your readers for the tone, subject, and content they will encounter in your research paper. It also tells them what kind of research you're going to cite. The thesis, which will often come at the end of your opening paragraph, is the place where you provide a succinct description of the opinion you're going to support in the body of the paper.

Thesis in Action Henri Bergson, a French philosopher, wrote an essay called "Laughter: An Essay on the Meaning of the Comic," which examines the human phenomenon of laughter. Bergson opens the first section of his essay this way:

> The first point . . . is that the comic does not exist outside the pale of what is strictly HUMAN. A landscape may be beautiful, charming and sublime, or insignificant and ugly; it will never be laughable. You may laugh at an animal, but only because you have detected in it some human attitude or expression. You may laugh at a hat, but what you are making fun of, in this case, is not the piece of felt or straw, but the shape that men have given it–the human caprice whose mould it has assumed.

We haven't gotten to a thesis yet. Bergson is warming up his readers with some examples they can relate to. He wants them to think, "It's true, I've never laughed at a landscape." He's setting them up for his thesis. Here's the next part:

> It is strange that so important a fact, and such a simple one too, has not attracted to a greater degree the attention of philosophers. Several have defined man as "an animal which laughs." They might equally well have defined him as an animal which is laughed at[.]

Here Bergson cites the research he will discuss. We know that he's examined the statements of philosophers and come to some conclusions about them. He concludes the opening this way:

> [I]f any other animal, or some lifeless object, produces the same effect, it is always because of some resemblance to man, of the stamp he gives it or the use he puts it to.

Finally, a thesis: we laugh only at what is human or what reminds us of humans. Bergson's thesis is controversial (he will have to prove that we would never laugh at the pratfall of a puppy, for example), it relies on research, and it is concisely stated.

Think Carefully

It's one thing to understand what a thesis is, but how are you going to come up with one? You should start by reading through all of your notes, so that the book you read first is as vivid in your mind as the article you just finished. Go back to your hypothesis and think about how your research has changed or confirmed that hypothesis.

Then, think. Coming up with a thesis is not a concrete, reading-and-taking-notes sort of process. Aspects of it can be physical—as you're thinking, you'll probably shuffle your note cards around, page through the books you've found most useful, and maybe jot down a few possibilities. But coming up with a thesis is really a matter of staring into space, or frowning down at your shoes, or assuming whatever position you're usually in when you're doing hard thinking. You should come up with three or four possible theses in your mind. Nearly always, the best thesis will "click" in your head, and you'll be able to imagine each supporting paragraph spiraling down from that thesis.

Then, and only then, should you pick up a pen, or turn on your computer, and start to write down the thesis, refining the language and getting the statement as concise and accurate as possible.

Know the Pitfalls

When you're coming up with a thesis for a research paper, the unfortunate fact is that many traps await you. It's much easier to create a weak thesis than it is to create a great one. There are several common pitfalls:

- Being "unopinionated"
- Having a too-broad focus
- Neglecting your research

Being "Unopinionated" Your take on your research can be interesting and well reasoned, but if it's one that nearly all reasonable people would immediately agree with then *it's not a thesis.* A good thesis makes some readers think, "Hmm . . . is that really true?" The paper then marshals evidence in a way that convinces readers the thesis is reasonable. When you're sitting down to create your thesis, think of yourself as a bit of a research-paper rebel. You don't want to rehash what other people have said or put a little spin on some piece of conventional wisdom. You want to shake things up and make people think.

- **Unsuccessful: The "Unopinionated" Thesis**

John Currin's controversial depiction of women has often overwhelmed discussions of his exquisite painterly technique.

On first glance, this thesis might look like a winner. It's well written, it points to the writer's research on art criticism, and it's clear and concise. The problem is that it's not actually a thesis, because even though it *mentions* controversy, it itself could not be called controversial. Nearly everyone would agree that the vast majority of articles on Currin have focused on his depiction of women, rather than on his artistry. Think of it this way: if your thesis could be proved correct with a Lexis Nexis search or a statistical analysis, it's a statement of fact, not a thesis.

- **Successful: The Opinionated Thesis**

By distracting critics with his controversial depiction of women, John Currin has managed to sneak in a revival of Velázquez-ian standards of technique under the critical radar.

This time around, the writer has kept the strengths of the unsuccessful thesis and added the key ingredient: an opinion. In this thesis, the writer shows that she has analyzed what critics say and come up with a theory: that Currin purposefully distracts attention from his true aim, which is to bring back high standards of technique. This thesis could be attacked from a number of directions. Readers might say, "Currin doesn't care about other painters' standards, only his own," or "Currin is wedded to his subject matter; it's not a means of distraction," or "Currin is mocking Velázquez, not imitating him," or "A return to technique is a recognized trend, not something that's under the radar." All of these potential attacks mean that the writer has done her job and come up with an opinionated thesis.

Having a Too-Broad Focus You've done lots of research, and you probably have tons of ideas swimming around in your head. If you're lucky, you've found many angles that interest you. Now you have to resist the temptation to incorporate several of your best ideas into one thesis. An overly broad or multifaceted thesis will mean ruin for your paper. It will force you to rush from point to point, get vague, and cram in all sorts of dubiously related research. You want to write an extremely thorough and controlled paper on just one manageable opinion. For most students, the mantra to repeat is: "Narrow your focus."

- **Unsuccessful: The Overly Ambitious Thesis**

Currin's paintings are preoccupied with mythology, informed by his personal relationships, and aggressively rebellious against art world fashions.

In this thesis, the writer displays a keen interest in the topic, which is great, but he bites off more than he can chew. Mythology, personal life, the art world—it's far too much to discuss thoroughly in under fifty pages. It also gives readers a sinking feeling that they're in for a wild, disorganized ride. You want to reassure your readers that you're going to home in on one aspect of your topic and take them through it step by step.

- **Successful: The Narrowed Thesis**

Currin's interest in mythology makes even his most controversial paintings more traditional than they are outrageous.

This thesis is a successful one. It concerns just one subject, refers to the writer's research on mythology and traditions in painting, and states the surprising opinion that Currin's paintings are, in the end, traditional. It also assures readers that the writer will be able to do a thorough exploration of his thesis, as opposed to a scattered and disorganized one.

Neglecting Your Research As you know, you're writing a research paper, not an essay. However, chances are that you have more experience with essays than you do with research papers. So one pitfall is that you'll come up with a thesis that is opinionated, concise, and original—all of the things a wonderful thesis should be—but that this thesis will be inappropriate for a research paper. Your thesis *must* rely on research. It *must* be informed by research. It *must not* be something you could convincingly argue without doing a lick of research.

- **Unsuccessful: The Nonresearch-Based Thesis**

Currin's art, while explicit, is often tender in its depiction of its nude subjects.

This is a strong thesis, but the writer could easily defend it simply by examining her own opinions of Currin's work. She does not need to cite interviews, articles, or books in order to support this thesis, which makes it inappropriate for a research paper.

- **Successful: The Research-Dependent Thesis**

The critics who rush to defend Currin's work from charges of misogyny wind up defending not Currin, but themselves from accusations of prissiness or shrillness.

This thesis is specific and opinionated, and it depends on research for its strength. The writer has clearly read criticism of Currin, has an opinion about it, and will discuss it in her paper.

Be Respectfully Bold

You might worry that your instructor will be annoyed by a thesis that challenges or contradicts something he or she said in class. However, the truth is that most teachers respect well-reasoned opinions, even if those opinions differ from their own. They want students to learn from their classes, but what they want even more is for students to develop critical thinking skills. If your paper is solidly argued, strongly analytical, and well written, your instructor will consider it successful, even if its thesis is precisely the opposite of what he or she argued in class. In fact, many instructors are impressed by students who are bold enough to make rebellious arguments.

Being Respectful Even though it's fine to be bold and even challenge your instructor, you shouldn't be disrespectful, intentionally shocking, or falsely rebellious. It might seem like a fine line between laudable efforts to be bold and distasteful efforts to shock, but it's easy to stay on the right side of that line by remembering the key: stay respectful. Think of yourself as an eager apprentice who has become expert enough to break away from an employer you respect and start your own business. You can challenge the dominant view while remaining deeply respectful of the scholars who hold that view. It's the difference between arguing that antidepressants are safe for teenagers in most cases and arguing that anyone who says teenagers shouldn't use antidepressants is an irresponsible idiot.

Disagree with Yourself

When you create your thesis, keep in mind that *you don't have to agree with yourself.* Making an argument that you yourself don't particularly agree with is a perfectly acceptable way to go. Let's say you're writing a research paper on Louisa May Alcott, and you feel that *Little Women* is her strongest work. After doing research, you find that several critics condemned the novel as sentimental and that Alcott herself disliked it for many reasons. Even though you still like *Little Women* better than the other Alcott novels you read over the course of your research, you decide to write a paper that focuses on some of the novel's weaknesses, even if you yourself don't actually think those weaknesses exist. Remember that your goal is to create a convincing argument supported by research—not necessarily to create an argument you support yourself.

Use Your Research

When you first set out to do research, you had a hypothesis in mind, a general theory you wanted to investigate. That hypothesis guided your research and determined which books, articles, and websites you explored. As you read, you kept an open mind and allowed your research to modify your original hypothesis as necessary. At this stage, you should *use* your research to refine your hypothesis and turn it into a thesis. Take a look at the sources you've gathered and the notes you took. These will help you to change your hypothesis into a thesis.

You'll find that your research has probably done one of three things to your hypothesis:

- Contradicted
- Modified
- Confirmed

Research Contradicted Your Hypothesis It's possible that your research wound up proving your original hypothesis wrong. If this is the case, it's not cause for panic. In fact, it's cause for congratulations. Like a professional researcher, you weren't wedded to your original idea. Now you're charged with the task of turning that original idea into a thesis. You already know you want to reverse the original hypothesis. Now you should think about exactly *how* your research changed your mind. In what ways did your research undermine your first idea? What were the most powerful arguments against your idea? It's in those arguments that you're likely to find your thesis. Take a look at this example:

Hypothesis: The personal life of Henry VIII was governed by politics.
Thesis: The marriages and divorces of Henry VIII were guided purely by desire, a policy that led to bloodshed and political disaster.

Research showed that it was desire, not politics, that affected the personal life of Henry VIII. We've revised our hypothesis, and our thesis reflects our new idea.

Research Modified Your Hypothesis In many cases, researchers find that their research does not prove their original hypothesis entirely right or entirely wrong; rather, it *modifies* their first idea. If this is the case for you, try to identify three or four ways in which you could rework your hypothesis, based on your research, in order to make it narrower and more accurate. What did your research confirm about your hypothesis? What did it disprove? Take a look at this example:

Hypothesis: Gelsey Kirkland was everything George Balanchine desired in his dancers.
Thesis: Gelsey Kirkland's off-stage clashes with George Balanchine eclipsed her physical and artistic excellence.

Our research showed us that we needed to modify our hypothesis to reflect a slightly different idea. Though Kirkland was indeed a wonderful dancer, our research showed us that her personal conflicts with Balanchine were actually more powerful in her career than her dancing skills.

Research Confirmed Your Hypothesis In this scenario, although you were on the alert for resources that would contradict or modify your original hypothesis, that hypothesis turned out to be confirmed in every significant way by your research. Even if this is the case, however, you still have work to do. Hypotheses are usually quite broad, and most are not controversial. In writing a thesis, you must narrow your hypothesis and push it. Think about what the most interesting facet of your research was. What surprised you? What did you read about with the most attention? Use your research to take your hypothesis to the next step. If your original hypothesis is true, what unique, focused idea do you have about that hypothesis?

> **Hypothesis:** Cats were worshipped as gods in Ancient Egypt.
> **Thesis:** The worship of cats in Ancient Egypt often endangered the lives of humans.

Our hypothesis, though correct, isn't very debatable—no one would really find anything to disagree with, and a research paper on this topic wouldn't be very interesting. By tweaking our hypothesis, we created a thesis that is more surprising and controversial.

Write the Thesis

You've stared into space, you've thought hard in the shower, you've ruminated on several possible theses, and you've chosen the best one. You have the argument all worked out in your head. Now it's time to get the thesis from your head onto paper or into your computer.

The thesis should always be the first part of the paper you write. Not the outline, not the opening paragraph—the thesis. The thesis is the hub of your essay from which everything radiates out. Writing it first will help you order your supporting paragraphs and figure out how to use your research most effectively. You can't write an outline and then go back and figure out what it all adds up to. If you do that, your paper will read like a transcription of your thought process, which is not interesting for your readers.

Staying Flexible It's entirely possible that you'll revise your thesis as you write your paper—it's not set in stone. It might be necessary to reword it so that it fits more smoothly into the opening paragraph, or, after writing a supporting paragraph or two, you might see that you need to change the focus slightly. You should feel free to fiddle with your thesis as your paper takes shape. Remember: your thesis isn't finished until your paper is.

Creating a Thesis in Action It's time to write a thesis for our paper on *Annie Hall*. Our original hypothesis was that psychological analysis, one of the key focuses of *Annie Hall*, turns out to be useless for Alvy Singer. This was a perfectly acceptable hypothesis and helped guide our research. However, it doesn't make the grade as a thesis. Here's why:

1. **It's "unopinionated."** Nearly every reasonable viewer of *Annie Hall* would agree that analysis doesn't do much

good for Alvy Singer. As we've discussed, papers that rely on uncontroversial theses are bound to be failures.

2. **It doesn't rely on research.** Nearly always, your hypothesis is something you come up with before you've gone to the library or searched for online sources. It makes sense, therefore, that most hypotheses don't rely on research. In our case, we came up with a hypothesis after seeing *Annie Hall*, but before reading any books or articles. The result was an idea we could easily defend simply by doing close analysis of one film—which is fine for an essay, but not acceptable for a research paper.

As we researched, we identified these two problems with our hypothesis. We also found that while we were still interested in psychological analysis, we were most interested in its effects on the title character of the film, Annie Hall. We wondered what women in 1970s' New York thought about analysis and whether Annie's was a typical success story. Returning to the library, we checked out books on feminist interpretations of Freud.

As we sit down to write the actual thesis, we come up with several possible ideas:

1. Annie Hall becomes confident as a result of analysis that Alvy Singer recommends.
2. It's ironic that analysis, which Alvy recommends for a reluctant Annie, is what gives Anne the confidence to leave Alvy.

3. Annie's success with analysis undermines the idea that Freud is sexist.
4. Woody Allen suggests that analysis works better for women than for men.

In the end, we decided to go with possibility #3. Here's why:

- **Possibility #1** is opinionated, but again, it's not appropriate for a research paper. It could be argued effectively simply by analyzing the film.

- **Possibility #2** is too obvious and too narrow. Not many readers would disagree with the idea that Alvy's push for analysis for Annie becomes ironic by the end of the film. Moreover, the idea is so specific that it couldn't support an entire paper.

- **Possibility #3** depends on research. It's not quite specific enough as it stands, but with some revising it will make a strong thesis.

- **Possibility #4** is far too broad for the scope of this paper. To argue it effectively, we would have to analyze several of Allen's films and do lots of research on analysis's proven results for men and women.

With possibility #3 in mind, we can draft a thesis for our paper:

In his film Annie Hall, *Woody Allen shows that it is women who benefit most from Freud's work—specifically, Freud's theories of psychoanalysis.*

This thesis is opinionated (readers could say it's not clear whether women or men benefit most), it relies on research (it's clear that we'll cite research on psychoanalysis), and it's concise. Our paper will take shape from here. Keep in mind that your thesis will develop as you write your paper. Additional research and new ideas might show you that your original thesis missed the mark or that there's a way to make it stronger. Again, your thesis isn't done until your paper is.

Making an Outline

Outlines are essentially road maps that organize your thoughts and research into a cohesive, structured whole. Outlines aren't just helpful; they're crucial. You've done lots of research, and you have hundreds of ideas, reasons, definitions, and pieces of evidence swimming around in your head. You can't just toss them together underneath your thesis and hope they'll make sense. Instead, you need to arrange them, see how they fit together, and eliminate anything that isn't logical, relevant, or effective.

6

When you have your road map—your outline—in front of you, you'll know exactly what to include in your paper and in what order. If you feel panicked at the sight of a blank computer screen, an outline will be your lifesaver. You won't have to worry about finding a way to start writing—you just need to look at your outline to figure out what comes first. If you start out with a strong plan for how to organize your paper logically, when it's time to write your first draft you can focus on the actual *writing*. Spending time on your outline will make writing a first draft immeasurably easier.

Break Down the Structure

Imagine that you're in a coffee shop with an argumentative friend. You've just announced your opinion, and your friend has said, "I don't know if I believe you. How can you justify that?" You take a deep breath and plunge into a long speech, ticking off your arguments on your fingers. Even if you've never analyzed them before, you probably have several techniques for changing the mind of your most skeptical friend. They likely include making a series of points that build up to a conclusion and using only your strongest evidence instead of boring your friend with every little piece of proof you can think of.

Writing an effective outline is similar to making a persuasive case in the coffee shop. The goals are the same: you want to support your main opinion by presenting a series of compelling arguments. And an outline can help you organize those arguments effectively. Nearly every successful research paper will follow the same basic outline. Let's take a look at its parts:

I. INTRODUCTION

A. Introduce your topic

B. Deliver your thesis statement

C. Provide a road map for your paper

II. BODY

A. First major supporting argument

1. Statement of argument
2. Reasoning and evidence

B. Second major supporting argument

1. Statement of argument
2. Reasoning and evidence

C. Third major supporting argument

1. Statement of argument
2. Reasoning and evidence

III. CONCLUSION

A. Transition to thesis restatement

B. Summary of arguments

C. A broader point

The **introduction** orients your readers, tells them the opinion you'll be defending in the body of your paper, and gives them a sense of the evidence you'll be citing. It will make up around 10 percent of your paper.

The **body** is the meat of your paper and will take up 75–90 percent of the space. In it you'll lay out your arguments and defend them with evidence gathered from your research. An important note: keep in mind that you won't always have three supporting arguments in the body of your paper. You may have more or fewer, depending on how long your paper is. Also, one supporting argument is not necessarily one paragraph in your paper—an argument may very well stretch out over several paragraphs. Within each major argument, you may have smaller, more minor arguments that support your thesis as well.

The **conclusion** refers back to your thesis, sums up your arguments, and broadens out to mention a question for future research or to put the thesis in a larger context. It will take up about 5–10 percent of your paper.

Outline the Introduction Last

Your introduction has to orient your readers, set the tone for your paper, and suggest that your arguments are going to be laid out in an orderly, easy-to-follow manner. Although the introduction is the first paragraph of your paper, during the outlining process, put it off until after you've worked on the body of the paper. There are two reasons for this suggestion:

1. The introduction is key, but the most important element in it is your thesis, and you've already written that.
2. You'll have a better idea of what you want to mention in the introduction after you've determined what your supporting arguments will cover.

Focus on the Body

In writing your outline, you'll spend almost all of your time thinking about the body of your paper. The body is the place where you get to wow your readers with the depth and organization of your research. It is *not* the place where you get to cram in every single idea, quotation, and piece of evidence you've gathered. If you give in to that impulse, your paper will be scattershot, show-offy, and unconvincing. Perhaps the most important part of writing an outline is figuring out how to *select* what research to use and deploy that research most effectively. *Quality* of evidence, not quantity, is what counts.

Supporting Argument Components Let's get back to the coffee shop. Suppose you were trying to convince your friend that Jane Austen writes better dialogue than any screenwriter working today. You might say, "First of all, she's great because she knows how funny awkward conversations are. Remember the strawberry scene in *Emma*, with Miss Bates? Emma's being mean, and Miss Bates doesn't get it at first, and then she does and she's embarrassed. The whole thing is so awful and realistic."

Each of your supporting arguments will work in exactly this way. You'll start by stating your *argument*, and then you'll back up that argument with *evidence*. In the coffee shop, your argument was that Austen is great "because she understands how funny awkward conversations are." To prove that argument, you cited specific evidence from the novel *Emma*—the strawberry scene. In the context of research papers, *argument* and *evidence* have specific meanings:

- **Argument:** An idea that supports your thesis. Your arguments will be the results of your research and analysis. They will be original and possibly abstract ideas.

- **Evidence:** The proof, garnered from your research, which you use to back up your arguments. Evidence can be direct quotations; properly credited summaries of other writers' arguments; facts and figures; or some combination of all three. They will be the concrete material that supports your abstract ideas.

Choose the Right Number

The number of supporting arguments in the body will depend on the length of your paper. If you're writing five to seven pages, three supporting arguments will probably be enough. If you're working on a ten- to twelve-page paper, you'll likely need around six supporting arguments. It might seem that the more supporting arguments you have, the more convincing your case will be. But since your instructor almost certainly gave you a page limit, this isn't true. If you try to squeeze six supporting arguments into a five-page paper, they'll wind up being just a few sentences each, and you'll have room for only one piece of evidence for each. Quick, superficial arguments like this are not going to help you prove your thesis. It's much more important to go into depth on three or four supporting arguments than to gloss over ten.

Select Your Arguments

To find the best supporting arguments to include in your outline, start by writing down your thesis. Underneath, write down a list of all the possible supporting arguments you can think of, leaving plenty of space underneath each one. It's okay if you write down more arguments than you think you'll use. Your outline can go through several drafts. In fact, it *should* go through several drafts as you shore up your arguments and figure out what evidence you want to include.

Next, gather all of the notes you took from your research. Sort them according to which argument they would best support. After you've done this, return to your outline.

Underneath each possible supporting argument, write down a brief description of the evidence you'd use to back it up.

Auditioning Your Arguments Now it's time to audition each argument. Look at your outline as objectively as possible in order to decide which arguments you should keep and which you should cut. Ask yourself the following questions about each one:

- Is this argument truly relevant to my thesis?
- Do I have plenty of supporting evidence to back up this argument?
- Is this argument crucial, or am I attached to it only because it would allow me to cite a great quotation/idea/argument I found?
- Does this argument fit well with the other arguments, or is it a departure?

The best arguments will be relevant, easy to support with evidence, crucial to the paper, and a good fit with your other arguments.

Selecting Arguments in Action Let's say you're writing a five-page paper about the Chicago Cubs. You have a thesis statement, you've done your research, and now you need to create an outline. First, you write down the thesis (which will appear in your introduction). Underneath it, you write down the possible arguments you could use to support your thesis. Take a look at the outline on the next page:

I. INTRODUCTION

A. Deliver your thesis statement: The Cubs have thrived financially because of, not in spite of, their years of failure.

II. BODY

A. First major supporting argument: Fans had a solid identity because of failure, spent money in droves.

1. Many fans passed down their fandom from generation to generation. Quote from several *Sun* interviewees: "I just want my grandfather to be alive to see the Cubs win."
2. Ticket prices soared every year (cite statistics), but fan attendance generally increased instead of decreased.
3. Appeal of showing your fandom even in other cities. Idea of Cubs fans as threatened minority. Huge profits on Cubs gear, cite stats re: popularity of gear compared to other teams.

B. Second major supporting argument: Constant media attention to failure built up mythos surrounding the team.

1. Every writer loved the Cubs failure story—cite *Slate* editor who moaned he couldn't stand one more writer who roots for the Cubs—adds up to pages and pages of free advertising.

2. Success of books like *The Curse of the Billy Goat* (quote sales figures) spurs more books of that kind, which leads to more fan attention, which leads to more ticket sales, etc.

C. Third major supporting argument: Built-in storyline—will the Cubs finally win this year?—led to national interest.
1. Cite number of times ESPN reporters mention the Cubs per show.
2. Cubs game as tourist attraction. Cite number of non-Cubs fans at each game.

D. Fourth major supporting argument: Focus on how Cubs's lovable screwups, not on their sizable budget, made team a fan favorite.
1. Cardinals characterized as evil moneybags leads to dwindling nat'l attention.
2. Cite number of times writers mention 1908 vs. number of times they mention that Cubs have a sizable operating budget.

After creating this outline, which includes four possible supporting arguments, you decide four arguments are too many for a five-page paper. It seems that the final argument is less crucial to your thesis than the others: it's really about the way the Cubs are characterized in the media, instead of about how their loser status led to profits. You decide to cut it and focus on the other three.

Organize Your Arguments

Once you've decided on the arguments you definitely need to support your thesis, think about how they should be arranged. The way you organize your supporting arguments is key to how successfully you defend your thesis. Try to put yourself in the mind of your readers: which progression of arguments would make *you* most willing to buy the thesis? There are three methods of organization that you should think about:

1. Strongest to weakest
2. Chronological
3. Logical flow

Strongest to Weakest When you have several different arguments to support your thesis, consider starting with your strongest argument and ending with your weakest. If your readers encounter a completely convincing argument in the first paragraph, you'll get them on your side, and they'll more inclined to go along with a more risky or surprising argument later on.

Chronological It's possible that there is a chronology built in to your thesis. Perhaps you're writing about a series of occurrences, a historical event, or a progression. If that's the case, your structure should mirror that chronology. Your readers will find it easier to follow an orderly progression that moves forward through time, rather than a series of arguments that jump back and forth.

Logical Flow Sometimes each argument will lead naturally to the next. Try to place each argument directly after the one it logically follows. If you separate related thoughts, even by just a paragraph, you'll sacrifice the logical momentum you're building in the mind of your readers.

Acknowledge the Other Side

If your paper is long enough, it's a great idea to devote some time to an acknowledgement of the other side of the debate. **Counterarguments** strengthen your paper because they show that you've considered opposing points of view and understand why people hold them.

It's best not to place counterarguments, no matter how compelling, near the beginning of your paper. You want to start out by telling readers why they should believe you, not by providing them with reasons to discount your arguments. Save the acknowledgment of counterarguments until near the end of your paper, before your conclusion.

Ponder the Conclusion

The conclusion is the place where you revisit your thesis, summarize the arguments you've made, and broaden your focus a bit. If you were writing a paper on how financial success of the Cubs rests, in part, on their "loser" status, for example, you might broaden out by saying, "The question now facing the Cubs, who have profited so handsomely from failure since 1908, is what will happen if they win. They may find that winning will cost them millions of dollars in the years to come."

The *broadening* requirement is usually the most challenging aspect of a conclusion, and it's a pretty hard requirement to fulfill before you've written a draft of your paper. For that reason, we advise holding off on detailing too much of your conclusion in the outlining stage. It's enough to get the bare bones of the conclusion—some thoughts or possibilities—down on paper.

Outlining in Action A completed outline involves figuring out what arguments to use and how all the pieces connect together to support your thesis. Here's our outline for our paper on *Annie Hall*.

I. INTRODUCTION

A. Introduce your topic (We'll do this later.)

B. Deliver your thesis statement: In his film Annie Hall, Woody Allen shows that it is women who benefit most from Freud's work–specifically, Freud's theories of psychoanalysis.

C. Provide a road map for your paper (We'll do this later too.)

II. BODY

A. First major supporting argument

1. **Statement of argument:** Many modern scholars agree with their 1970s' counterparts that Freud's theories are quite sexist.

2. Reasoning and evidence

a. Modern scholars view Freud's theories as misogynist (quote Chodorow).

b. Freud angered many feminists in the 1970s (quote Dimen).

B. Second major supporting argument

1. **Statement of argument:** In Annie Hall, Woody Allen turns this conventional wisdom on its head, arguing that psychoanalysis is immensely useful for women and practically useless for men.

2. **Reasoning and evidence**

   a. Explain Allen's own experience in analysis; many years, few results

   b. Alvy's jokes about fifteen years, going to Lourdes, lobster bib—basically he makes fun of the uselessness of his analytic experience

C. Third major supporting argument

1. **Statement of argument:** Annie is a self-loathing girl when she embarks on her relationship with Alvy, and an independent woman when it ends—all thanks to analysis.

2. **Reasoning and evidence**

   a. Annie's pre-analysis stuttering (quote tennis dialogue) reveals her deep insecurity.

   b. Because of analysis, Annie gains confidence and speaks clearly and strongly. Mention her familiarity with and reliance on terms she's picked up in therapy.

D. Fourth major supporting argument

1. **Statement of argument:** Annie explores her own past and psyche in analysis, whereas Alvy doesn't get much done in analysis.
2. **Reasoning and evidence**
   a. Analysis of Frank Sinatra dream
   b. Refusal to sleep with Alvy—courage to do that based on what she's learned in therapy
   c. Alvy's jealousy over Annie's first session. She accomplishes more in one day that he's accomplished in fifteen years.
   d. Poor analysis of Frank Sinatra dream

E. Fifth major supporting argument

1. **Statement of argument:** Analysis gives Annie tools she can use in the real world, whereas it gives Alvy no tools.
2. **Reasoning and evidence**
   a. Strength during the breakup
   b. Rejection of marriage proposal
   c. In contrast, Alvy's desperate marriage proposal
   d. Alvy's rebellious behavior toward the cop. He knows the terms, but can't put them to use.

III. CONCLUSION

A. Transition to thesis restatement

B. Summary of arguments

C. A broader point

(We'll write the conclusion when we write our first draft.)

Our outline gives us a strong structure for our paper. To begin, we're going to discuss the conventional wisdom surrounding Freud, whose theories were considered sexist both in the 1970s and today. After explaining the standard thinking, we're going to show how Woody Allen undermines it in his film by arguing that analysis can work wonders for women such as Annie. To highlight the success of Annie's experience in analysis, we're going to contrast her improvement with Alvy's total lack of improvement. This back-and-forth analysis of Annie and Alvy will comprise the bulk of our paper.

You'll notice that we've piled up five major arguments. We might be overdoing it, and it's likely that some of these arguments will be combined and others deleted. But note that it's always better to be overly detailed than overly vague. Additionally, it's better to give yourself too much material to work with, rather than not enough. As we write this outline, all of the ideas included seem crucial to the paper. This might not hold true as we write and revise, but for now, we're planning to explore each one and see what works.

You might find this outline a little cryptic. Your outline will probably be equally hard for an outsider to decipher. This is fine and even desirable. Don't forget that *you* are the only audience for your outline. It's best to get all your ideas down on paper without interrupting the flow of your thoughts to write complete sentences. Your outline might look like a bunch of chicken scratches, but as long as it's legible to you and gives you a road map to your first draft, it's doing its job.

Writing a First Draft

When you were assigned your research paper, you may have thought you had two stages ahead of you: researching and writing. But now you can see how many steps there are before the writing even begins. If you haphazardly gather some sources and stuff facts and quotes into a paper, you won't have an argument—you'll have a mess. Writing a first draft isn't as rough as you might think, but it is the culmination of a lot of careful work.

If you've faithfully followed our recommended steps so far, we have good news: the hard part is over. Even if you dread writing, you'll find that your preliminary work has made this process much easier. You've thought, planned, hypothesized, researched, come up with your thesis, and outlined. Everything you need for your first draft is already at your fingertips. Instead of staring at a blank page and wondering where on earth to start, you'll know exactly where you're going—and how to begin.

Start Early

You might be tempted to put off the actual writing until the last minute, but this could undo all of your hard work. No matter how thorough your research, it will be useless if you don't showcase it in a carefully written paper.

You should strive to finish writing your first draft *at least* two days before your paper is due. The key is to give yourself time to finish the draft, get a good night's sleep, go about your day, and then return to the draft with fresh eyes. That short time away from your work allows you to see exactly how your paper should be revised and reorganized. The revision stage of the writing process is integral to creating an excellent research paper: you can't skip this step if you want a high grade. The best tactic is to write your first draft quite early on so that you can come back to it many times before handing it in. This kind of preparedness might seem impossible to pull off, but if you try it once, your work will improve so much that you'll never procrastinate again.

Stay Focused

It used to be that students settled down to write by opening a notebook or putting a fresh sheet of paper in the typewriter. In those days, the distractions were ringing telephones or random daydreams—interruptions that were outside the immediate workspace. But these days, the very place where you work is full of distractions. As soon as you open up Word, someone IMs you; an icon pops up announcing the arrival of new email; or you get to wondering whether your favorite blogger has posted anything new in the last five minutes.

To stay focused and make effective use of your time, rid yourself of these temptations. Promise yourself that for a full hour—or half hour, whatever is reasonable for you—you won't do anything other than work on your draft. No IMing, no emailing, no poking around the internet. Then, after you've focused for that promised stretch of time, allow yourself to take a break.

Have Faith in Your Outline

You should always *trust your outline* as you write. If you come to an argument that seems confusing or that gets garbled when you try to write it out, try to retrace your mental steps. What thought process led you to that initial idea for an argument? In most cases, there's nothing wrong with your outline. You just need to remember what you were thinking originally. If you decide you want to rethink aspects of your outline, that's fine—your outline is yours to tinker with. Returning to your outline might feel like taking a step backward, but it's just a way of firming up your foundation before you move on.

Your outline is the skeleton of your paper. When you write the first draft, you're putting flesh on those bones. There are three ways you'll turn your outline into a paper:

1. **Expanding** your sketched-out arguments and evidence into full-fledged sentences and paragraphs
2. **Adding** material to clarify your thoughts
3. **Connecting** each point to the next with transitions

Expanding Expanding the ideas, evidence, and comments that you put in your outline into fully fleshed-out sentences and paragraphs is key to using your outline effectively. Far from a random list of ideas, your outline is a logical, carefully planned road map for your paper. If you've outlined painstakingly, you can simply expand on each and every element in your outline and come out with a decent first draft.

Adding As you create a paper from your outline, you may have new ideas or find gaps where you need to do more research. Don't be afraid to add material to your outline as you go along—this is a natural part of the writing process.

Connecting Simply making full sentences out of thoughts and phrases won't yield an excellent paper—rather, you'll have a group of unrelated thoughts. Though the connections between your ideas are probably very clear to you, the writer, you must take care to be explicit in your paper as to how your ideas build and relate to one another. Your readers will be approaching your material for the first time—they need some guidance from you as they go along.

Focus on Ideas, Not Style

You want your paper to be a pleasure to read, a symphony of flowing paragraphs, elegant sentences, and perfect word choices. Great—but now is *not* the time to think about that. As you're writing your first draft, don't lose momentum by consulting your thesaurus or dictionary or by rewriting each sentence until it's perfect. The most important task now is to get your ideas down on paper. Focus on the clarity and connection of those ideas, rather than on the elegance with which they're expressed. You'll have time to polish later, during the revision process.

Marking Minutiae When you write your first draft, you should focus on ideas and connections between ideas, not on Minutiae. For that reason, you should come up with a system for marking places you need to come back to or facts you need to check. You can put [brackets] around questionable spots, *italicize* them, put them in **bold font**, surround them *with asterisks*, or use whatever other method works for you. When it's time to revise, you won't forget to go back to these places and take care of the details.

Avoiding Academia-ese Your first draft will be both difficult to write and hard to revise if your prose is the windy, overblown academia-ese that many students use when writing papers. It's a mistake to think that your instructor will be impressed by sentences such as, "Refusal to attempt understanding often leads to conflict, whilst striving to overcome stereotypical notions and achieve open-mindedness oftentimes engenders cooperation." He or she *will* be impressed by a sentence such as, "Close-minded thinking leads to conflict, while open-minded thinking leads to cooperation."

In your first draft, strive for the kind of straight-ahead, uncomplicated prose you might read in *Newsweek*. It is possible—and desirable—to express complex ideas in a simple way. It's also easier to focus on expressing your ideas and getting them down on paper if you're not busy trying to sound fancy. Believe it or not, you will sound much smarter if you strive for simplicity instead of resorting to abstractions, wordiness, and jargon.

Draft the Introduction

Your introduction is the place where you orient your readers and draw them in. It sets them up for what they will encounter in the body of the paper, and it establishes you as a credible, interesting, and knowledgeable guide. It's the place where you make a first impression.

Think about the way news articles begin. Many of them lure the reader with a colorful anecdote or quotation that leads directly to the story. You're writing an academic paper, so your approach will be a little different, but the principle is the same: you want to simultaneously let readers know what your topic is and get them interested in that topic. You don't want to begin by saying, "This paper will discuss the important, if relatively narrow, topic of the multinational corporations, international organizations, and collective dependence on interdependence of industrialized nations." Openings like this will make your reader's eyes glaze over in boredom. Instead, provide some background information that shows why your topic is important and interesting.

Think of your introductory paragraph as an upside-down triangle:

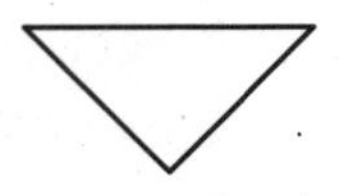

It begins broadly and narrows down to a point: your thesis.

Starting Big and Narrowing Down The first three or four sentences of your introduction should exceed the scope of your paper. However, you shouldn't start *too* broadly. If you're writing a paper on the battle of Gettysburg, for example, things will get out of hand if you begin by discussing the Pilgrims' arrival to America or Abraham Lincoln's childhood. Exceeding the scope of your paper means discussing your topic in general before you get to your thesis in particular. For the Gettysburg paper, you might begin with a few sentences about the state of the Confederate Army in the months before Gettysburg or a recap of the key battles in the war prior to Gettysburg.

In deciding where to begin your introduction, it will help to think back to the first stages of your research, before you had narrowed your focus. What about your topic initially piqued your interest? How did you form your hypothesis? What fascinated you will likely fascinate your readers.

After the brief discussion of your topic, narrow down to the specific issue you have researched. You want to ground your readers and steer them toward your thesis, which will come near the end of your introduction.

Mentioning Research The introduction should make it clear to the readers that you will rely on research to prove your thesis. However, there is no need to say, "I formed my thesis after reading *The Guns of August*." It's fine to mention a few of your key sources in the introduction, but be sure to weave them into your prose, rather than shoving them in the reader's face. For example, you might write, "The concept of élan is key to an understanding of war, as *The Guns of August* and other works suggest."

Don't feel pressure to enumerate your sources in the introduction. If it feels easy and natural to work them in, great; if not, you have plenty of space to get to them later, in the body of your paper. The suggestion that your paper will draw on research—something like "Many theorists discuss the importance of élan among troops"—is just fine for the introduction.

Introducing Your Arguments After you've started broadly and narrowed down to your thesis, write a few sentences that lay out the arguments you will make to back up your thesis. Think of these sentences as a road map for your readers. If they know what to expect, they can relax and enjoy your paper.

Length Your introduction will make up around 10 percent of your paper. If you're writing a five- to seven-page paper, this means your introduction should be around three-quarters of a page. Try to keep your introduction down to one healthy paragraph. If you're writing a longer introduction, you may have to break it up into two paragraphs. In that case, confine your broader material to the first paragraph, and introduce your thesis and your road map in the second.

Introduction in Action We're going to take a stab at drafting the introduction to our paper on *Annie Hall*:

> By 1977, when <u>Annie Hall</u> was released, Freud and his ideas were firmly entrenched in Manhattan's cultural imagination. As ?? Associate Professor of Psychoanalytic

Studies at Australia's Deakin University writes, "psychoanalysis permeated American intellectual life, especially in New York." But not all privileged Manhattanites embraced Freud; feminists objected to him and his theories in the strongest terms. In his film Annie Hall, Woody Allen shows that it is in fact women who benefit most from Freud's work—specifically, Freud's theories of psychoanalysis.

This introduction begins broadly, with a sentence about Freud's prominence in Manhattan during the time of *Annie Hall's* release. To add credibility to that assertion, we quote a professor. Following the upside-down triangle format, we narrow down to a statement about the way New Yorkers, specifically feminists, felt about Freud. Finally, we narrow down still further and reach our thesis statement.

Note the two question marks (??); we use them to mark places that will need attention during the revision process. In this case, the question marks point to a missing name. This quotation is from an online source that we copied and pasted into a Word document. Due to sloppy note-taking, we lost the name of the professor in question. Finding the name shouldn't be difficult, since we can Google the quotation. At the same time, hunting for names is exactly the kind of potentially distracting task that shouldn't be undertaken during the draft-writing process. The question marks are our way of saying, "Come back to this trouble spot later."

Draft the Body

The body of your paper is where you'll support your thesis using the evidence you've gathered. It is the meat of your paper. Because you've written an outline, you have a pretty good idea of the way each paragraph in the body will work. What remains now is to flesh out your ideas, make sure each argument connects logically to the next, and deploy your research in the most effective way possible.

Each paragraph should address just *one* key point. While your paper should weave many arguments together into a cohesive whole, it's not a good idea to refer backward to arguments you have made and forward to arguments you will make in the space of one paragraph. Instead, focus on one argument per paragraph. Keep in mind that it's fine if an argument stretches out over more than one paragraph. Sometimes a particular argument will require more substantial exploration.

Topic Sentences In the body of your paper, topic sentences must do a lot of work. Ideally, someone should be able to read only your thesis and the first sentence of each paragraph and *still* have a strong sense of what your paper argues. Topic sentences have two key jobs to perform.

1. Topic sentences must transition from the preceding paragraph.

It's important not to jump from one argument to the next without showing your readers how the two relate. So topic sentences must make the transition from argument to argument. Never assume that your readers will be willing to make logical leaps with you, or that they will figure out how two arguments relate to one another without being told. Instead, imagine that you are the expert and that you must explain your ideas to someone who is bright and attentive, but knows nothing about your thesis. Transitions are a way of taking your readers by the hand and guiding them through your paper.

Despite their huge importance, transitions can be very small. In fact, sometimes all that's needed is a phrase like, "Another method of oppression . . ." or "In a related incidence . . ." In some cases, you'll need a longer phrase, such as "After focusing on Aztec rituals of sacrifice, it is important to consider . . ."

The best papers are those in which each paragraph transitions naturally to the next. If you find that you're having a hard time getting your topic sentence to do transitional work, you might need to reexamine your outline to make sure that you've ordered your arguments in the most logical way.

2. Topic sentences must reveal the point of the paragraph they introduce.

If you put off revealing your argument, your readers will feel unsure of where you're going. They will likely rush through your paragraph without paying close attention to the sources you're citing in an effort to discover what point you're trying to make. If you explain the point right away in the topic sentence, your readers can relax and consider each piece of evidence you provide in support of that point.

The revelation of each paragraph's argument should be concise and accurate. You might write, "Another method of oppression is censorship, which silences the voice of anti-government groups," or "In a related scenario, a newlywed disappeared from a Carnival cruise without explanation," or "After focusing on Aztec rituals of sacrifice, it is important to consider their peaceful rituals, such as marriage ceremonies."

Incorporating Research The body of your paper is the place where you'll use research to support your thesis. Remember, a research paper is very different from an essay. Your thesis is an original argument, as it is in an essay, but here you are backing up that thesis with evidence drawn from sources, instead of your opinions. The topic sentence of each paragraph states an argument you are making based on research, and that argument must be supported by the most relevant, interesting, and convincing information you've found. Here's how to use all of that great information:

- **Sort Your Notes:** Before you start writing the body, go through your note cards or electronic notes and identify the arguments each note relates to most closely. Sort your notes into piles based on which note belongs with which argument. Then go through each pile and order the notes from most useful to least useful. The notes on the top should be quotations and evidence that you're certain you want to use; the ones on the bottom should be those that you don't think you'll end up using. This order can change as you're writing, but it will help you to approach each argument with a game plan.

- **Order:** You need to help readers understand your logic. One way to accomplish this is to order your evidence in the most logical way possible. If you're discussing the way critics have interpreted Ophelia over the years, it makes the most sense to start with the critic writing in 1915 and wind up with the critic writing in 2005.

- **Link:** A way to help readers move through your order is to link each piece of evidence to the next. These links function in exactly the same way your first-sentence transitions do. After quoting an article that condemns filibusters, for example, you might introduce a quotation that supports filibusters by writing, "Brendan Sullivan, however, believes that the opposite is true." Or if you've just summarized someone's argument, you can link it to a quotation by writing, "This is a view that the artists of the day found upsetting." Such a sentence alerts the readers that you're going to prove that the view was upsetting by quoting an artist.

- **Analyze:** In order for a reader to fully interpret your logic, you must analyze evidence before or after presenting it. Instead of flinging a quotation into a paragraph and hoping your reader will understand how it relates to your argument, introduce it by saying something such as, "In a 1976 interview, Smith was surly and uncommunicative." Or, depending on the way your paragraph is unfolding, it might work better to do the analysis after citing your source. If you've just summarized a writer's argument, you might interpret for the reader with a sentence such as, "This position became the conventional wisdom in the 1980s."

- **Cite, but Don't Obsess:** You might feel a little anxious about the ins and outs of citing sources in your paper. But at this point, don't worry too much about the correct citation methods. As always, it's crucial to keep track of which source you're quoting, paraphrasing, or summarizing, so be sure to put the title of each source next to the citation in parenthesis, followed by the page number from the source. But you don't need to make the format of every citation perfect at this point. You'll do that in the revision process.

Length The body will comprise 75 to 90 percent of your paper. Ideally, no one argument will eclipse another in size or scale. You don't want one argument that takes three pages to be followed by another argument that you make in one short paragraph. An imbalance like that will suggest that you haven't modulated your ideas carefully, didn't do enough research, or simply ran out of time. Your arguments don't need to be precisely the same length, but they should be roughly comparable.

In your first draft, you don't need to think too much about how your arguments match up. The most important task is to get all of them down on paper. Later, you can add or subtract material as needed.

Body in Action Take a look at this paragraph from our first draft of our *Annie Hall* paper:

> Annie is a self-loathing girl when she embarks on her relationship with Alvy, and an independent woman when it ends—all thanks to analysis. When she first meets Alvy, Annie can hardly form a complete sentence without savagely mocking herself. After Alvy contemplates her tennis skills, saying she plays well, Annie responds,
>
> > "Oh, yeah? So do you. Oh, God, what a—what a dumb thing to say, right? I mean, you say it, 'You play well,' and right away, I have to say you play well. Oh, oh . . . God, Annie. Well . . . oh, well . . . la-di-da, la-di-da, la-la."
>
> At the end of this agonizing speech, Annie comes close to linguistic breakdown, abandoning adult English for nonsense songs. When she invites Alvy to her apartment, she spends most of the visit babbling nervously and wondering if she's too dumb to date him. In many scenes, she allows Alvy to mock her for her quaint, girlish "Chippewa Falls expressions," which he finds first endearing and then annoying. Because of analysis, Annie's voice changes from weak, stuttering, and meandering to strong, precise, and cutting. Instead of enduring Alvy's mockery, Annie is able to match wits with him. When he uses a Freudian term in his defense, saying, "I've got to see a picture exactly from the start to the finish, 'cause . . . 'cause I'm anal," Annie fires back with the assuredness of someone who has mastered

the concepts: "Ha, that's a polite word for what you are." Waiting in line for a movie, Annie again relies on the vocabulary of analysis to express herself, telling Alvy, "You know, you're so egocentric that if I miss my therapy you can only think of it in terms of how it affects you!" These pointed, quick-witted remarks contrast strikingly with the nervous, fumbling speech that Annie uses before entering analysis.

The first sentence of this paragraph follows our key topic sentence rule: explain the point of the paragraph. Right away, we let readers know that they're going to hear about the way therapy changes Annie's character. Next, we paint a "before" picture of a nervous, insecure Annie by quoting dialogue from the film. Note that instead of launching into a quotation with no explanation, we set the scene ("After Alvy contemplates her tennis skills, saying she plays well . . ."). We also do a little analysis of the quotation ("linguistic breakdown") rather than rushing away from it to the next point. By bookending the tennis dialogue with our own thoughts, we're making our reasons for including this particular quotation clear to the reader. More examples of Annie's self-consciousness follow. We note her nervousness during Alvy's visit and her willingness to let him tease her about her Chippewa Falls expressions.

So far, we've fleshed out the first part of the topic sentence ("Annie is a self-loathing girl when she embarks on her relationship with Alvy"). Now we turn to the second part ("[Annie is] an independent woman when it ends"). A sentence of analysis makes the transition. In this sentence, we call Annie's pre-analysis voice "weak, stuttering, and meandering" and contrast it to her post-analysis voice, which we call "strong, precise, and cutting." To back up this analysis, we cite the way Annie uses Freudian terms to match wits with Alvy, quoting the scene in which the couple go to a movie. Finally, we sum up the paragraph with a final sentence that underlines the striking difference between Annie's pre- and post-analysis self.

This paragraph is quite long and will need to be trimmed or divided into two during the revision process. But it's a great start. Remember, it's always better to have too much material to work with than too little.

Draft the Conclusion

The concluding paragraph of your paper, like the introduction, should resemble a triangle. This time, however, the triangle is right side up:

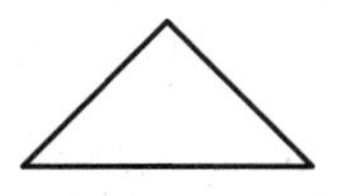

The conclusion should start with a tight focus on your paper and then widen out to encompass a broader perspective. You want to stress how important your topic is, and briefly touching on the wider implications of the topic is a good way to do that.

Expanding the Scope There's no one right way to broaden out, but here are a few suggestions to get you started:

- **Go from local to universal:** If you're writing about an aspect of one culture, time period, or country, think about how the issues you've discussed related to other cultures, time periods, or countries. If your paper addresses the practice of foot-binding, for example, your conclusion might mention ways women in other countries are physically abused under the guise of tradition.

- **Relate to modern times:** Your paper might explore an event, trend, or person from the past. Think about what relevance that topic has to our own time. If your paper is about religious hysteria and the Salem witch trials, your conclusion could make reference to religious beliefs that some feel are endangering parts of the world today.

- **Consider a question for future research:** Think back to your research process. Were there any avenues you wished you could explore? Your broadened perspective could bring up the possibility of further research. If you've written a paper on the importance of soccer to Mexican national identity, your concluding paragraph could suggest investigating the importance of soccer to other Latin and South American countries.

Your conclusion should not tackle an entirely new topic; the bulk of it should refer back to your thesis and supporting arguments. The purpose of broadening out is simply to show that you've considered how your topic fits into a wider context.

Length Your conclusion should make up just 5 to 10 percent of your paper. It's not the place to do any heavy lifting. Like a light dessert after a full meal, it should leave a pleasant taste in your reader's mouth. To this end, don't summarize everything you argued in your paper. This will bore your reader and waste space.

Conclusion in Action Let's take a look at the drafted final paragraph of our *Annie Hall* paper:

> In Annie Hall, Allen makes the case that in contrast to what feminist critics believe, psychoanalysis is not misogynist. On the contrary, he suggests that it is of great use to women. By contrasting Annie's wonderful experience with Alvy's terrible one, he argues that analysis can transform an awkward girl into an independent woman. One critic writes, "Individuals such as Woody Allen are constantly searching for ways to get rid of intolerable feelings and, like most artists, to put them into their work." (James). Perhaps Allen has done just that in Annie Hall.

This paragraph will need some work in revision, but it's perfectly acceptable as a first-draft effort. In its first three sentences, it sums up the main argument of the paper. Then it begins to broaden outward, following the triangle model. We use a quotation from a British critic to make the transition from summary to broader scope. The quotation observes a link between the "work" of artists like Allen (film such as *Annie Hall*) and the personal feelings of those artists. In the final sentence, we suggest that Allen has gotten "rid of intolerable feelings" by making *Annie Hall*.

Don't Stop Now

When you write a first draft of a research paper, you have to focus on presenting your ideas clearly and logically. However, you have another goal as well: to incorporate sources smoothly, effectively, and correctly. Unlike in an essay, where you have to worry about only your own thoughts and arguments, in a research paper you have to add outside sources into the mix. In Chapter 8, "Incorporating Sources," and Chapter 9, "Citing Sources," we'll tell you everything you need to know about how to use sources in your paper. And in Chapter 11, "Model Research Paper in Action," we give you a complete first draft of our paper on *Annie Hall* to show you how it all comes together.

Incorporating Sources

You've already combed the internet, trolled the stacks, done the reading, made the notes, and incorporated those notes into your outline and draft. In terms of research, all of the mental heavy lifting is over. But even if you've spent days in the library and read thousands of sources, all your hard work won't pay off unless you take the time to present your research intelligently.

8

Think of your paper as a tapestry and yourself as the weaver. Most of the thread in your tapestry will consist of your own opinions and conclusions. Woven throughout will also be the thread of your research. If you do your job well, the threads will come together to make an elegant, tightly woven pattern. In other words, it's not enough for the research to just *be there*. There's an art to incorporating sources.

Know When to Use What

Take a look at your note cards: each one should be labeled Quotation, Paraphrase, Basic Fact, and so on. These note cards will be invaluable tools as you pick and choose the sources you want to cite in your paper. However, while you have a lot of choices about what information to include, you have only *two* choices when deciding *how* to include it: quote or paraphrase. Often, a Quotation note card will translate into a quotation in your paper. But you don't have to feel bound by the way you originally classified information. Don't worry if, as you write, you decide that a quotation should actually be a paraphrase, or vice versa. Try to stay mentally flexible as you sort through your note cards, and think carefully about how you want to incorporate your research.

Quoting Many students writing research papers for the first time fill each page with quotation upon quotation. Leaning on the experts is a great impulse, and adding their voices to your own can be a good way to build your argument. However, there are many times when a direct quote *isn't* necessary. In order to deserve inclusion in your paper, each phrase, sentence, or passage quoted should be succinct, beautifully worded, and original. If you find that your rough draft is overstuffed with quotations, put each one to the test:

- **Is It Succinct?** If you could compress the quotation significantly while retaining all of its meaning, consider doing so.

- **Is It Uniquely Worded?** Each quotation you include should be a pleasure for your reader to encounter. If the language of the original source is pedestrian, boring, or filled with jargon, it's not worth quoting. However, keep in mind that sometimes the very dullness of the quotation may prove your point, so think carefully before you automatically delete it.

- **Is It Original?** Ideally, each quotation in your paper will enlighten, amuse, or demystify something for your reader. Try your best to include the most interesting and original quotations from each source.

Paraphrasing It's possible that when you began doing research, you didn't know much about your subject. In contrast, the people whose books and articles you read were impressively well versed on the topic. When it comes time to incorporate their ideas and arguments into your paper, you might feel timid about paraphrasing them rather than quoting in full. They're the experts, right? Shouldn't you simply quote what they've written instead of putting it in your own words? To be blunt: no.

Experts' arguments have several possible problems, which can include that they are:

- Too long-winded for your purposes
- Worded confusingly
- Hard to incorporate into your paragraph because of grammatical issues
- Simply not fun to read

If you find that an expert's argument has one of these problems, your best bet is to paraphrase that argument—always followed, of course, by a proper citation. When you paraphrase an author's argument, keep the following rules in mind.

- **Stay true to the author's meaning.** Don't modify the author's meaning at all, and don't include any of your own opinions in the paraphrase.

- **Keep to the general length of the original passage.** If the original passage is two sentences, your paraphrase shouldn't consist of five sentences or of three words. In most cases, it should be the same length or slightly shorter than the original.

- **Don't include any direct quotations.** If you feel you must quote a few words, be sure to put them in quotation marks. Even though you'll cite the author and page number at the end of the paraphrase, it's dishonest to use one of the author's exact phrases without making it clear to the reader that the phrase is not your own.

Paraphrasing in Action In the first draft of our paper on *Annie Hall* (see Chapter 11), we quote an article by Oliver James from the online version of the United Kingdom newspaper *The Times*. Our original quotation looks like this:

> One critic writes, "Individuals such as Woody Allen are constantly searching for ways to get rid of intolerable feelings and, like most artists, to put them into their work" (James).

While the ideas James discusses are interesting, we decided that the prose he used wasn't particularly exciting or succinct and therefore not worth quoting at such length. Instead, it seemed best to paraphrase:

Critic Oliver James suggests that artists like Woody Allen want both to expunge their neuroses and to use those neuroses in their art.

This paraphrase follows all the rules: it stays true to James's meaning, it's around the same length as the original, and it doesn't quote James directly. (Note that since this information comes from an online source, no page numbers are necessary.)

Balance Research and Opinion

Your own ideas and arguments are just as important as the research you cite. It might seem like a good idea to cram as many quotations, paraphrases, and facts as possible into each paragraph since, after all, you're writing a *research* paper. But this isn't the best strategy. While it's important to use as much outside information as you can, it's also important to make your own arguments the glue that holds that information together.

In the body of your paper, each paragraph should contain around 30 to 40 percent research and around 60 to 70 percent argument or opinion. In some paragraphs, the balance will be more like 50-50. Ultimately, this paper should be *your own* argument *supported* by outside sources. While your readers will be interested in the research you've done, they will be most interested in your take on that research and in how you've put other writers' opinions and quotations together to bolster your thesis.

Guiding Your Readers Think of your readers as willing, intelligent people who know nothing about your topic. Paragraphs consisting only of quotation after quotation or paraphrase after paraphrase are dangerous because they will bore and confuse your readers. They'll wonder what all these sources add up to, what point they support, and why you've chosen to include those particular sources as opposed to others. Instead of testing your readers' patience with strings of quotations or paraphrases, *do all the work for them.* Tell your readers exactly how they should interpret the material from your outside sources.

Balancing Research and Opinion in Action Take a look at a paragraph that simply strings quotations and paraphrases together, without any input from the writer about what the research adds up to:

> Marriage was a problem for Balanchine. Karin von Aroldingen says that Balanchine referred to her husband as "'your other half or 'your better half'" (qtd. in Mason 498). Balanchine humiliated Farrell's husband at rehearsals, and eventually he asked Farrell to leave the company (Farrell 187).

This paragraph proves that its writer has done research, but that's just about all it accomplishes. It raises several questions: why did Balanchine oppose marriage? Why did he refuse to say the name of Aroldingen's husband? Why did he ask Farrell to leave the company? But it answers none of them. It's hard to figure out how the quotation and the paraphrase relate to the vague first sentence of the paragraph, or why they were included rather than other material from the writer's research. And it's impossible to identify the writer's interpretation of this material. Here is an improved version of that paragraph:

> Balanchine's genuine affection for his dancers and his conviction that married life ruined them made marriage not just a potential step away from the company, but an act of disobedience and betrayal. He notoriously scolded nearly every married woman in his company, from lowly corps member to prima ballerina, for her wedded state. Karin von Aroldingen says that Balanchine refused to speak her husband's name for four years, referring to him instead as "'your other half' or 'your better half'" (qtd. in Mason 498). The much-publicized marriage of Suzanne Farrell offended Balanchine deeply. Hurt by what he saw as her betrayal of him and his antimarriage stance, he humiliated her husband at rehearsals and eventually asked Farrell to leave the company (Farrell 187).

This paragraph provides context for the sources it cites. It starts out with a strong topic sentence that reveals the point of the paragraph: because Balanchine loved his dancers and believed that married life hurt them, he viewed marriage as a betrayal. The writer presents Aroldingen's quotation as an example of Balanchine's tendency to scold married women in his company. The writer also makes it clear that Balanchine asked Farrell to leave the company because he felt betrayed by her marriage. In short, this paragraph succeeds because it does all of the interpretive work for the readers.

Introduce Your Sources

Remember that your readers haven't been doing research along with you, and that only you know who your sources are. The first time you name a source in your paper, use his or her first and last name, and explain briefly who the person is by giving the source's occupation or credentials. By citing your source's credentials, you show your reader that the source is trustworthy. The more information you give your readers, the better. Take a look at these two examples:

> **INEFFECTIVE:** "Ed Said argues . . ."

You might know that Ed Said was a famous professor from Columbia University, but your readers won't understand why you're quoting this person, or even who on earth he is.

> **EFFECTIVE:** "Ed Said, who was a well-known professor of Middle East studies at Columbia University, writes . . ."

This introduction makes clear why you're including this particular source and shows he's a respected authority. You can also introduce a source by simply adding a short label, such as "Writer Raymond Carver . . ." or "Critic Pauline Kael . . . ."

Note that after you introduce your source the first time, you can and should use only the source's last name in the rest of the paper.

Avoid "Dropped" Quotes

A "dropped" quote is a quotation that appears in your paper with no introduction or explanation. Even if you're quoting a complete sentence or sentences, you still need to link that quotation to your own argument. Take a look at this dropped quote:

> **DROPPED:** "Another charge which some readers have made is that Lolita is anti-American" (315).

This quotation is interesting, but because no context is provided, its impact is lost. It raises too many questions: where did the quotation come from—a book, an article, an interview? Who wrote it or said it? Is it from a trustworthy source? Readers will spend more time wondering what critic, professor, or writer provided this quotation than what it means and why it's important.

To avoid dropped quotes, use a **signal phrase**. A signal phrase is a mini-introduction that puts your quotation in context. Look at how a signal phrase improves our example:

> **CORRECT:** In his afterword to Lolita, novelist Vladimir Nabokov writes, "Another charge which some readers have made is that Lolita is anti-American" (315).

Note how much information the writer is able to get across in that signal phrase. We now know the location of the quotation (the afterword of *Lolita*), the source's occupation (novelist), and the source's name (Vladimir Nabokov).

Long Source Titles In some cases, the source title might be too long to fit comfortably into your paper. That's fine; you'll cite the full title in your works cited or references list. But you should still use a brief signal phrase, such as "Nabokov explains . . ." or "According to critic Andrew Smith . . . ."

Be Grammatically Correct

Each sentence of your research paper should be grammatically impeccable—including sentences that include research. Make sure you work quotations smoothly into your paper, rather than simply tossing them in. Take a look at this example:

> **UNGRAMMATICAL:** Britain swore it would oppose him, "Hitler did not believe or did not fear the threat" (Keegan 41).

This is a run-on sentence. The phrases before and after the comma are both independent clauses (they are both full sentences). There are several ways to revise this excerpt to make it grammatically correct:

> **REVISION #1:** Although Britain swore it would oppose him, "Hitler did not believe or did not fear the threat" (Keegan 41).
>
> **REVISION #2:** "Hitler did not believe or did not fear the threat" that Britain made against him (Keegan 41).

> **REVISION #3:** According to Keegan, "Hitler did not believe or did not fear the threat" that Britain made against him (41).

In all of the revisions, we still include the quotation, but the sentence as a whole is grammatically correct. If you're struggling to make a quotation fit grammatically into a sentence, or if a pronoun taken out of context becomes unclear, don't despair. It's perfectly fine to make certain changes to the original material, as long as you signal to the reader that you've made those changes. You can use brackets or ellipses to indicate altered material.

Brackets If you need to change the case of a letter, or insert or replace a word, put brackets around the changed text:

> **ORIGINAL:** According to Keegan, "His divisions had been reduced by heavy fighting and long traverses of endless road" (193).
> **ALTERED:** According to Keegan, "[Guderian's] divisions had been reduced by heavy fighting and long traverses of endless road" (193).

> **ORIGINAL:** Because of the setbacks, "His confidence remained weakened" (Keegan 467).
> **ALTERED:** Because of the setbacks, "[h]is confidence remained weakened" (Keegan 467).

Ellipses Ellipses are useful in solving grammatical issues and compressing quotations. Use them when you want to include part, but not all, of a sentence or paragraph. Three dots indicate that part of a sentence has been removed:

> **ORIGINAL:** As Keegan notes, "German purchase of French, Dutch and Belgian industrial products–which included items for military use such as aero-engines and radio equipment, as well as finished steel and unprocessed raw materials–were acquired in a rigged market" (283).
> **THREE-DOT ELLIPSES:** As Keegan notes, "German purchase of French, Dutch and Belgian industrial products . . . were acquired in a rigged market" (283).

Four dots indicate that an entire sentence has been removed. Note that the first dot is *not* preceded by a space:

> **ORIGINAL:** According to Keegan, "Within exactly five minutes, between 10:25 and 10:30, the whole course of the war in the Pacific had been reversed. The First Air Fleet, its magnificent ships, modern aircraft and superb pilots, had been devastated. And the disaster was not at an end" (278).
> **FOUR-DOT ELLIPSES:** According to Keegan, "Within exactly five minutes, between 10:25 and 10:30, the whole course of the war in the Pacific had been reversed. . . . And the disaster was not at an end" (278).

Note that if you begin quoting in the middle of a sentence, rather than from the beginning, you *do not need to include opening ellipses* to indicate that text has been omitted.

Citing Sources

The art of incorporating sources goes hand in hand with *citing* sources. You'll face many challenges when writing a research paper, and citing sources correctly may be the biggest one. Citation comes with its own set of guidelines and rules, and the penalties for deviating from them are stiff: fail to cite correctly and you could face charges of plagiarism. All the best research in the world won't matter if you don't cite your research correctly.

Fortunately, the fact that citation guidelines are so black-and-white is ultimately good for you as a writer. All the guidelines might seem overwhelming, but you don't have to memorize them. With citation, nothing is left to chance, and all you have to do is follow the rules. We'll give you everything you need to know about citation and the most popular documentation styles so that you have these rules at your fingertips as you create your draft.

Place Citations Carefully

As you work, it's very important to avoid plagiarism scrupulously, and you know you need to cite every quotation and paraphrase you include. However, even if you'd never dream of stealing someone else's work, you might *unintentionally* mislead your readers into thinking someone else's words or thoughts are your own if you don't cite your sources properly. You must be extremely detail-oriented when it comes to citation. Suppose you're writing a paper on Catholic saints, and you begin a paragraph with these sentences:

> Early Christians believed that they themselves were all holy, even saintly. Still, from the first century on they recognized the exemplary importance of people "who, in imitation of Christ, had demonstrated outstanding holiness by dying for their faith" (Hallam 6).

Because of the placement of the citation at the end of these lines, readers would assume that only the last phrase in quotation marks comes from the source, a book by Elizabeth Hallam called *Saints: Who They Are and How They Help You.* In fact, the *entire point* is a paraphrase of a paragraph from page 6 of the book. Even if you're making a good-faith effort to cite your sources, mistakes like these can undermine your credibility and in some cases even lead to charges of plagiarism.

To avoid such errors, be absolutely clear about what material comes from you and what material comes from your sources. One way to accomplish this is to put the author's name at the *beginning* of a paragraph to indicate that a paraphrase is coming. For example, you could revise the above lines this way:

> In her book *Saints: Who They Are and How They Help You,* Elizabeth Hallam suggests that early Christians believed they themselves to be holy, even saintly. Still, she says, from the first century on they recognized the exemplary importance of people "who, in imitation of Christ, had demonstrated outstanding holiness by dying for their faith" (6).

Don't Cite Common Knowledge

One important aspect of citation is figuring out when it is necessary and when it is not. You know it's crucial to cite direct quotations and paraphrases, but what about the kind of information you wrote down on your Basic Fact note cards, such as essential info about dates, places, ideas, and so on? Information that is considered *common knowledge* does *not* need to be cited. For a fact or idea to be considered common knowledge, it must be one of the following:

- **Appropriate for a reference book.** Common knowledge (CK) is something you could look up in a dictionary, encyclopedia, or atlas.

  CK: Columbus sailed for America in 1492.
  Not CK: A theory about Columbus's personal motivation for exploring.

- **Widely known.** If a smart, reasonably educated person would know the information, it is common knowledge.

  CK: We know little about Shakespeare's life.
  Not CK: Shakespeare's marital situation.

- **Often referenced.** A piece of information that is referenced in every single source you've found is almost certainly common knowledge.

CK: Balanchine had romantic feelings for Suzanne Farrell.

Not CK: The reason Balanchine and Suzanne Farrell never married.

While you can get a good idea of the definition, there is no black-and-white rule for determining what is common knowledge and what isn't. When in doubt, provide a citation. It's *always* better to be overly explicit than it is to plagiarize.

Understand MLA Documentation Style

The Modern Language Association (MLA) has created a detailed set of guidelines for citing sources in certain types of academic papers. You'll likely use MLA style if you're writing a paper for a humanities class such as history, art history, English, journalism, and so on. It is the style we've used in our example citations in our paper on *Annie Hall*, as well as in the examples from this chapter. MLA documentation style has two main components:

- **In-text citations:** Citations that appear directly after the quotation or paraphrase in your paper. In-text citations generally consist of the author's last name and page number in parentheses, like this: (Hemingway 23). You will not use footnotes if you are using MLA style.
- **Works cited list:** A detailed list of all your sources that appears at the end of your paper. The entries in your

works cited list will include the author's name, the title of the work, publication information, and any other information that will enable readers to locate the source.

We'll explain in-text citations and the works cited list in detail. There are a lot of rules, but no one expects you to memorize them. Rather, you should keep this book handy and refer to it when it's time to cite your sources and create your works cited list.

Learn MLA Style

When you cite sources, you need to be as thorough and as careful as possible. Citing carefully will add credibility to your work, since you'll seem like a responsible, knowledgeable writer. When creating an in-text citation, pay close attention to what type of source you're using. Then find that source in the list that follows to see how to cite the source in your paper.

A works cited list includes much more detailed information about every source you used in your research paper. Your works cited list should *not* include every single source you came across as you researched your topic. It should include *only* those sources you actually referred to in your paper. A good rule of thumb: anything that appears in your paper should appear in your works cited list, and vice versa. As with in-text citations, there are a lot of rules about how to create works cited entries for your sources. Once you locate the type of source in the following list, however, plugging in the information is a cinch.

We can't possibly list every type of source here, so if you can't find what you're looking for, consult an MLA style guide or ask your instructor for help. What follows are the basics.

Basic Format Basic MLA citations for quotations and paraphrases consist of the author's last name and the page number enclosed in parentheses. No comma is used between the name and the number.

In-text citation:

As one writer notes, "If I am lukewarm about the dahlia, I am red hot about the bearded iris" (White 97).

If the author's name appears in a signal phrase, you don't need to put the name in parentheses.

In-text citation:

As author Katharine S. White notes, "If I am lukewarm about the dahlia, I am red hot about the bearded iris" (97).

A basic works-cited entry includes the author's name, the title of the work, place of publication, publisher, and publication year.

Works cited entry:

White, Katharine S. Onward and Upward in the Garden.
Boston: Beacon Press, 2002.

Underline titles of books, journals, newspapers, films, and plays. Use quotation marks for articles, stories, lectures, and poems.

Source with Unknown Author If no author is identified for your source, put a short form of the source's title in the parentheses, along with a page number.

In-text citation:

Some critics complain that nonunionized teachers assistants take out their frustration on students ("Union Blues" A4).

In your works cited list, the title will appear first. It's important that whatever you put in the parentheses matches the works cited entry.

Works cited entry:

"Union Blues." Editorial. Student Daily. 8 Nov. 1995: A4.

Source with Two or More Authors When a source has two or three authors, both authors' names should appear in the parentheses.

In-text citation:

Robert Newton has been called "the rubber-faced actor best remembered for his role in the fifties' remake of Treasure Island" (Buhle and Wagner 203).

Note that in the works cited list, the first author only should be listed last name first. The other author should be listed first name first, last name last.

Works cited entry:

Buhle, Paul, and Dave Wagner. Blacklisted: The Film

Lover's Guide to the Hollywood Blacklist. New York: Palgrave Macmillan, 2003.

When a source has four or more authors, use the phrase *et al.* in your parentheses (Latin for "and others").

In-text citation:

In Alphabet Soup, a novel theory of alphabetic order is put forward (Tucker et al. 114).

In your works cited list, list only the first author last name first.

Works cited entry:

Tucker, Taylor, et al. Alphabet Soup. Akron: Ice Press, 2001.

One Author, Two Sources If you use two different sources by the same author in your paper, you must be clear about which source you're quoting or paraphrasing from. Use a short form of the source's title along with the author's name and page number.

In-text citation:

The food theme appears almost immediately in this article by Leah Amis ("Time" D1). In an article appearing the same week, however, Amis focuses entirely on travel ("Revealed" A2).

If you need to list two or more works by the same author in your works cited list, list the author's name only once. After that, indicate the name with three dashes followed by a period.

Works cited entries:

Amis, Leah. "Time for Thai." Harpers Gazette 15 May 1999: D1.

"Travel Perils Revealed." Harpers Gazette 20 May 1999: A2.

Source in an Anthology If you cite one work from an anthology, cite the page number and the author of that work, *not* the editor(s) of the anthology.

In-text citation: (Quoting from a story that appears in The Best American Short Stories of the Century):

Andrea "was sure that the bowl brought her luck" (Beattie 596).

In your works cited list, provide the full information about the anthology and its editor(s). But list the work by the author's, not the editor's, name, and include page numbers.

Works cited entry:

Beattie, Ann. "Janus." The Best American Short Stories of the Century. Ed. John Updike and Katrina Kenison. New York: Houghton Mifflin, 1999. 595–599.

Work in Translation When citing a work that has been translated, provide the translator's name in the text if it's not too awkward.

In-text citation:

McGuinness's interpretation of Ibsen's play A Doll's House is a feminist one. For the majority of the play, Torvald treats Nora with kind condescension. In the first scene, he says, "But nothing my lovely, little Nora . . . My little bird that fritters is so very fragile, but she does waste an awful lot of money" (I.i).

In the works cited list, order the entry according to the author's last name. Place the translator's name, first name first, after the title of the work.

Works cited entry:

Ibsen, Henrik. A Doll's House. Trans. Frank McGuinness. London: Faber & Faber, 1996.

Source within a Source Occasionally you'll want to include a quotation or an argument cited in another work. In this case, you must indicate the work in which the quotation or argument appeared.

In-text citation:

Karin von Aroldingen says that Balanchine refused to speak her husband's name for four years, referring to him instead as "'your other half' or 'your better half'" (qtd. in Mason 498).

The interview with Aroldingen appeared in a book by Francis Mason.

Works cited entry:

Mason, Francis, ed. I Remember Balanchine. Pennsylvania: Diane Publishing Company, 1991.

Magazine Article Magazines articles should be cited in your text as you would cite a book.

In-text citation:

"Where," asks writer Brittany Thoreau, "have all the career-focused mothers gone?" (23)

Order your works-cited entry by the author name. Also include the article's title, the magazine's name, the date of publication, and the page numbers.

Works cited entry:

Thoreau, Brittany. "The Opt-Out Epidemic." Manhattan Mother Jan. 2004: 23–26.

Newspaper Article Newspaper articles should be cited in your text as you would cite a book. Be sure to include both a section letter and page number.

In-text citation:

Trillon examines the songs most frequently chosen for inclusion in compilation CDs (C12).

In the works cited list, order the entry by the author's name, followed by the article's title, the newspaper, the city of origin if it is not apparent, the date, and the section letter and page number. If the article appears on nonconsecutive pages, indicate it with a plus sign after the page number.

Works cited entry:

Trillon, Cedric. "Now That's What I Call Narrow." College World [Boston, MA]. 3 Dec. 2000: C12+.

Pagination If you are referencing books, magazines, journals, or other source materials with numbered pages, include the relevant page numbers in your parenthetical citation. If you're citing more than one page, include the range.

In-text citation:

Author Bill Hotchkiss takes the opposite stance (20–21).

Sometimes you'll need to cite newspaper or magazine articles that run on nonconsecutive pages. Suppose the article above begins on page 20, continues to page 21, and then leaps to page 138. Indicate this in your works cited list with a plus sign.

Works cited entry:

Hotchkiss, Bill. "Bullfighting Reconsidered." Men's Style 20 Jan. 2003: 20+.

Some journals **paginate by issue**. That is, each issue begins at page 1. In your works cited list, provide the volume number followed by the issue number and the page numbers.

In-text citation:

Nils Brown, professor of anthropology, investigates the courtship rituals of penguins living in captivity (145).

Works cited entry:

Brown, Nils. "Restrained and Selected." American Anthropology 20.4 (2004): 145–152.

Some journals **paginate by volume**. That is, they number their pages as if each journal were going to be put together to make one book, rather than restarting each issue at page 1. In your works cited list, provide the volume number, year, and page numbers.

In-text citation:

Wilson discusses women's portrayal as objects used in ritual dances (240).

Works cited entry:

Wilson, Wendy. "From Totem to Talisman: Women in Ritual." Hourly Review 12 (1999): 240–300.

Interviews, Lectures, Songs In certain cases, such as when you're quoting an interview, lecture, or song, citing a page number will be impossible. Instead of putting a name by itself in parentheses, cite the source by explaining it in the text itself.

In-text citation:

Professor Mizruchi suggested in her lecture that The Catcher in the Rye can be read as a long cry of mourning.

Works cited entry:

Mizruchi, Susan. Lecture. 1 Oct. 2005.

In-text citation:

In his song "Kick in the Door," Notorious B.I.G. begins with a sample that sums up his ethos: "I've got to talk. I've got to tell what I feel. I've got to talk about my life as I see it."

Works cited entry:

B.I.G., Notorious. "Kick in the Door." Disc 1. Life After Death. Bad Boy, 1997.

Literature, Plays, Poems In your paper and in your workscited list, underline the titles of books and plays and put the titles of short stories and poems in quotation marks. Note that when citing plays, it's more useful to list act and scene numbers rather than page numbers, since pagination will vary depending on the edition and translation your reader is using.

In-text citation:

In the first act of Shakespeare's Othello, Desdemona asserts that her first allegiance is not to her father, but to her husband. She addresses her father, saying, "here's my husband, / And so much duty as my mother showed / To you, preferring you before her father", she must show equal duty to her own husband (I.iii.184–186).

Note that in the works cited entry below, the "2nd ed." after the play's title indicates that this is the second edition of Penguin's *Othello.*

Works cited entry:

Shakespeare, William. Othello. 2nd ed. New York: Penguin Putnam, 1996.

Websites Because most websites don't provide page numbers, you can't include them in your citations. Mention the appropriate website in the text, and include the author's name, if known, in parentheses.

In-text citation:

Gawker.com reported on the proclivities of the publishing criminal (Coen).

In your works cited list, provide as much of the following information as possible, in this order:

- The author's name
- The material's title
- The website's title
- The names of the editor(s)
- The publication date or last update
- The name of the sponsoring organization
- The date you accessed the site
- The URL in angle brackets

Titles of entire websites or book-length material should be underlined; titles of entries, posts, poems, stories, articles, and so on should be placed in quotation marks and followed by the title of the website.

Works cited entries:

Nolan, Hamilton. "Individuality Is a New Luxury Automobile." Gawker. Ed. Nick Denton. 25 Feb. 2008. 1 March 2008 <http://www.gawker.com/news/>.

Ward, Celeste. "Venti Coffee with a Double Shot of Annoying." Adfreak. 1 Dec. 2005. 25 Feb. 2008 <http://adweek.blogs.com/>.

Websites with Unknown Author Many websites are written anonymously. If this is the case for a source you're citing, leave out the author's name, while providing all of the other relevant information you can.

In-text citation:

The engineering page at Columbia.edu mentions the many patents held by engineering faculty members.

Works cited entry:

Columbia Engineering. Dec. 2005. Engineering Dept., Columbia University. 5 May 2008. <http://www.studentaffairs.columbia.edu/admissions/engineering/>.

Websites with an Editor Editors' names should be cited following the website's title and the author's name, if any, in the works cited list.

In-text citation:

"Greatest Movie Ever?" is typical of Goldenfiddle.com's spare, sardonic posts.

Works cited entry:

"Greatest Movie Ever?" Goldenfiddle. Ed. Spencer Sloan. December 2005. 14 April 2008. <http://www.golden fiddle.com/>.

Websites with a Group Author If no one author is identified, cite the official source of the information. Be as specific as possible.

In-text citation:

The United States government publishes online transcripts of press secretaries' conferences, including McClellan's October 24 conference.

Works cited entry:

United States. White House. Press Briefing by Scott Mc Clellan. 2 Dec. 2005. 24 Oct. 2007. <http://www.white-house.gov/news/releases/2005/10/20051024-3.html>.

Online Material with No Title If the online material you're citing isn't titled, simply describe the type of material cited (homepage, website, blog, etc.) in the works cited list.

In-text citation:

Information about the singer Diana Krall can be found on her official website.

Works cited entry:

Krall, Diana. Official website. 14 June 2004. 25 Dec. 2007. <http://dianakrall.com>.

Online Library Resources Citation rules for such services as *EBSCOhost*, *InfoTrac*, and *ProQuest* are similar to citation rules governing websites.

In-text citation:

Terry McCarthy examines the vigilante groups patrolling America's borders (36).

In your works cited list, provide as much of the following information as possible, in this order:

- The author's name
- The material's title
- The names of the editor(s)
- The publication date or last update
- The name of the sponsoring organization
- The name of the database
- The name of the service
- The place (name and location) where you accessed the article
- The date you accessed the article
- The service's URL in angle brackets

Works cited entry:

McCarthy, Terry. "Stalking the Day Laborers." Time. 5 Dec. 2005: 36. InfoTrac. New York Public Library, New

York. 20 Dec. 2005. <http://web6.infotrac.
galegroup.com/>.

Learn MLA Style: Other Rules

MLA style involves more than just rules for in-text citations and works cited lists. There are also some general guidelines for the way you write your paper. As you become more familiar with writing research papers, these guidelines will become second nature.

Verb Tense Use the present tense when referring to what your sources say.

> **INCORRECT:** In her book *Onward and Upward in the Garden*, Katharine S. White **wrote**, "Color and form and hardiness are the thing" (71).

> **CORRECT:** In her book *Onward and Upward in the Garden*, Katharine S. White **writes**, "Color and form and hardiness are the thing" (71).

Punctuation Periods go outside the closing parenthesis for in-text citations. If you're quoting something that includes a quotation, the quotation marks in the original text turn into single quotation marks in your paper. The following sentence illustrates both rules:

> Ehrenreich points out, "There are German tourists who are so touched by my pidgin *'Wilkommen'* and *'Ist alles gut?'* that they actually tip" (19).

If the original sentence ends in a question mark or an exclamation point, keep that *inside* the closing quotation mark. The citation in parentheses comes after that, with no period after it:

> According to Ehrenreich, "If he's so rich, I can't help wondering, then why is he driving this rusty old wreck and how come his front teeth are so scraggly and sparse?" (65)

If you want to include a semicolon in the middle of a sentence, after a quotation, put the page number here:

> Ehrenreich writes, "The Superwoman mood does not last" (86); this change is mainly due to her physical discomfort.

Format for Long Quotations Quotations of four or more lines should be indented by about five spaces, or one tab. These quotations are called **block quotes**. A few of the basic punctuation rules don't apply in this case: don't use quotation marks around the indented material, and place the final punctuation mark before the opening parenthesis, not after the closing parenthesis. Here's an example:

> At the beginning of Chapter 10, Vladimir introduces the Fifth Avenue apartment, with its European feeling and its desirable location:
>
>> Not to mention the quiet graces of the family that came with this geography: the Ruoccos feasting, constantly feasting from the "gourmet garages" that were

> taking the town by storm. An avalanche of peppercorns and stuffed grape leaves in handsome containers, resting on real tables (the kind with four legs) on which candles were always lit and above which chandeliers glowed faintly on dimmers. (Shteyngart 85)

Notice that there are no quotation marks around the quotation, and the citation at the end comes *after* the period. Also, note that the entire excerpt is double spaced, with no extra space before the block quote.

Poetry Short quotations of one or two lines of poetry can be included in your text. To indicate line breaks, insert a slash surrounded by spaces:

> Dickinson writes, "There is a Languor of the Life / More imminent than Pain–" (152).

Quotations of three lines or more should be indented or centered. As with longer quotations from prose, the closing punctuation of the quotation should be placed before the opening parenthesis of the citation. And everything should be double spaced:

> In these lines, the narrator cites her half-lived life:
>
> That I did always love
> I bring thee Proof
> That till I loved
> I never lived–Enough–(Dickinson 226)

Learn MLA Style: Paper Format

Formatting your paper according to MLA standards is another signal to your readers that you've done careful, thorough work. Here are the basic guidelines.

Materials

- Use standard 8½" x 11" white paper.
- Paper clip the pages (do not staple).

First Page

- No title page is necessary.
- In the upper left-hand corner, include the following on separate lines, in this order: your name, your instructor's name, course title, and date of paper submission.
- Title should be centered above the body of the paper.
- Your last name and the page number should appear in the upper right-hand corner of every page, one-half inch below the top of the paper.

Margins

- Use one-inch margins on all sides.
- Left-align your paper—don't center the text.

Spacing

- Double-space your entire paper, including any block quotes.
- Don't add extra space between the title and the body, or between paragraphs.
- Indent each opening sentence five spaces (one-half inch).

Works Cited

- Begin the list on a new page at the end of the paper.
- Center the words *Works Cited* above the list.
- Double-space each entry.
- Capitalize all the words in a title except prepositions, articles, and conjunctions (*a*, *and*, etc.).
- Do not include *page* or *p.* when citing page numbers. Simply put the numbers.
- Alphabetize by authors' or editors' last names.
- List author's and editor's last name first, first name last. When listing more than one, do this only for the first name.
- Separate multiple authors with commas.
- If no author exists, alphabetize by title (ignore articles such as A and *The*).
- If you're listing more than one work by the same author, use "--- " in place of the author's name in all entries except the first. Alphabetize by the title of the work.
- Don't indent unless the entry runs for more than one line. In that case, indent the additional lines five spaces.
- Remove hyperlinks.

Understand APA Documentation Style

Like the MLA, the American Psychological Association (APA) has its own set of citation guidelines. You'll likely be asked to follow these guidelines if you're taking a class in the social sciences (such as psychology or sociology) and sometimes business. Just as with MLA style, it's important to follow APA style closely and carefully. Doing so will make your paper professional and credible.

Just as with MLA style, APA documentation style involves two parts:

- **In-text citations:** Citations that appear in parentheses and include the author's last name, the date of the publication, and sometimes the page number.
- **List of references:** A list of all the sources included in the paper, giving all the relevant publication information of each.

We'll explain APA citations and the references list in detail. Don't worry about trying to memorize all the details. Even writers who have written many research papers often need to refer back to the documentation rules.

Learn APA Style

Details count when you cite sources. Careful documentation will make your paper more convincing, and you'll avoid all potential issues with plagiarism. When creating an in-text citation in APA style, pay close attention to the type of source you're using. Then find that source in the following list to see how to cite the source in your paper. At the end of your paper, you should include a list of references. The format for a source's entry in the references list depends on what type of source you're using. Follow the guidelines we've provided here to figure out how to create your references list.

We can't possibly list every type of source, so if you can't find what you're looking for, consult an APA style guide or ask your instructor for help. What follows are the basics.

Basic Format Most APA citations consist of a signal phrase introducing the author, directly followed by the year of the source's publication enclosed in parentheses. If the citation is a direct quotation, page numbers are also included. Use *p.* for one page and *pp.* for more than one page. Use commas to separate these elements.

In-text citation:

According to Mary Ann Glendon (1991), "[T]he opinion in the *DeShaney* case miseducates the public about the American version of the welfare state" (p. 97).

If you're paraphrasing rather than quoting, no page number is necessary.

In-text citation:

Glendon (1991) analyzes the *DeShaney* case in some detail.

In your references list, put the author's last name first, a comma, the author's initial or initials, and the date in parentheses. Italicize book titles, newspaper names, and magazine names; put article and chapter titles in regular roman font.

References list entry:

Glendon, M.A. (1991). *Rights talk: the impoverishment of political discourse.* New York: Free Press.

Source with Unknown Author When the author is unknown, put the source title in your signal phrase; alternatively, you may mention a shortened version of the title in parentheses.

In-text citation:

United Nations: Confronting the Challenge of a Global Society (2004) examines the question of the U.N.'s role in the modern world.

In-text citation:

The question is: what is the U.N.'s role in the modern world? (*United Nations*, 2004).

In the references list, alphabetize by the source's title. Note that when citing book titles in the references list, the first word only of the title is capitalized. (In this case, both are capitalized because "United Nations" is a proper noun.)

References list entry:

United Nations: confronting the challenge of a global society. (2004). London: Lynne Reinner Publishers.

Source with Two or More Authors Both authors must be named either in parentheses or in a signal phrase every time you cite the work. Use an ampersand between the names in parentheses.

In-text citation:

This relates to the authors' discussion of "self theorists" (Hill & Kral, 2003, p. 13).

Use the word *and* between the names in the text.

In-text citation:

This relates to Hill and Kral's (2003) discussion of "self theorists" (p. 13).

Sources with up to six authors should be listed by last name, first initial for each author. If the source is written by more than six people, list the first six authors followed by the words *et al* (Latin for "and others").

References list entry:

Hill, D.B., & Kral, M. (2003). *About psychology: essays at the crossroads of history, theory, and philosophy.* Albany: State University of New York Press.

One Author, Two Sources You'll be able to distinguish between works by the same author by listing the date of publication. If the works are published in the same year, distinguish between them using lowercase letters.

In-text citation:

Aaronson (2005a) discusses the effect of divorce on grandchildren.

In your references list, repeat the author's name for each entry. Order the entries from earliest publication date to latest publication date. If the date of publication is the same, order alphabetically by title and use the lowercase letters you used in the text of your paper.

References list entries:

Aaronson, L. (2005a, May/June). The long arm of divorce. *Psychology Today.*

Aaronson, L. (2005b, May/June). The pleasures of life's uncertainties. *Psychology Today.*

Two Sources, One Set of Parentheses If you need to list two references in one set of parentheses, order them as they will be ordered in the references list, and separate them with semicolons.

In-text citation:

Authors tackle the intersection of theory and quantification (Caspari & Wolpoff, 1998; Lewin, 1997).

References list entries:

Caspari, R. & Wolpoff, M. (1998). *Race and human evolution: a fatal attraction.* Boulder, Colorado: Westview Press.

Lewin, R. (1997). *Bones of contention: controversies in the search for human origins.* Chicago: The University of Chicago Press.

Work in an Anthology In your paper, cite the author of the specific article or chapter you're referencing, rather than the editor of the anthology. If you're citing Geoffrey Bennington's chapter in an anthology edited by Carol Sanders, it might look like this:

In-text citation:

Bennington points out that Derrida's approach to Saussure is *not* that of "a professional linguist" (p. 186).

In your references list, start with the author's name, rather than the editor's. Include the editor's name in parentheses after the book title.

References list entry:

Bennington, G. (2004). Saussure and Derrida. (Sanders, C., Ed.) *Cambridge companion to Saussere.*

Source within a Source When citing a quotation or argument you found in another source, use the signal phrase to mention the original source.

In-text citation:

According to Derrida, language is "essentially vocal" (as cited in Bennington, 2004, p. 187).

List the *secondary* source (not the original source) in your references list.

References list entry:

Bennington, G. (2004). Saussure and Derrida. (Sanders, C., Ed.) *Cambridge companion to Saussere.*

Magazine Article Cite magazine articles in your text as you would cite any other reference.

In-text citation:

Professor Nehry (1992) wants her analysands to examine their own craving for analysis.

In your references list, note the exact date of publication. Note the volume number, if one exists, in italics after the title.

References list entry:

Nehry, L. (1995, May 30). Irreparable harm: the pop-culture depiction of analysis. *Psychology Now*, 25, 46–52.

Newspaper Article If you are citing an article that appears on consecutive pages, give the exact page number in the text and the range in the references list.

In-text citation:

Editorial writer Yvette Garcia (1992) uses the captor/prisoner experiment as an example of "the rapidity with which we internalize the roles society hands to us" (*Student Bugle*, p. 5).

In the references list, the exact date is required. Page numbers are preceded by *p.* or *pp.*

References list entry:

Garcia, Y. (1992, July 1). Brutality and its practitioners. *Student Bugle*, pp. 5–6.

Pagination APA style puts more emphasis on providing dates than on providing page numbers for the sources you're citing. While it's crucial to provide page numbers for direct quotations, you are not required to provide page numbers for paraphrases.

If you are citing an article that appears on **consecutive pages**, give the exact page number in the text (if you're quoting) and the range in the references list.

In-text citation:

Vaughn Whitfield (1980) cites the handbook's overwhelming influence (*Student Bugle*).

References list entry:

Whitfield, V. (1980, Nov. 15). Forever prep. *Student Bugle*, pp. A2–A3.

If the article appears on **nonconsecutive pages**, give the exact page number in the text (if you're quoting) and all pages in the references list.

In-text citation:

Violet Stark's (1980) response foreshadows a goth rebellion (*Student Bugle*).

References list entry:

Stark, V. (1980, Nov. 22). Studs, spikes, and ennui. *Student Bugle*, pp.B7, C3.

Some journals **paginate by issue**. That is, each issue begins at page 1. In your references page, note the volume number (italicized) followed by the issue number (not italicized) in parentheses.

In-text citation:

Professor Bloomfield (2001) expresses his views in typically outrageous language.

References list entry:

Bloomfield, H. Whither Lacan? *The Monthly Review*, *21* (10), 25–30.

Some journals **paginate by volume**. That is, they number their pages as if each journal were going to be put together to make one book, rather than restarting each issue at page 1. In your references list, provide the journal's title and volume number, both in italics. Also provide the page number(s).

In-text citation:

Rachel Friedberg (2003) takes on the general state of the profession.

References list entry:

Friedberg, R. The state of the science. *Sociology Today*, 44, 217–229.

Interviews and Lectures In your paper, cite interviews, lectures, and other in-person source materials like this:

In-text citation:

For all of the thousands of articles and books written on the topic, essentially scholars are mystified by the question of why we dream (P. Lynn, psychology department chair, November 1, 1997).

Do not include such sources in your references list.

Internet Sources When using APA style to cite internet sources, the general rule is to make your in-text citations resemble, as closely as possible, your citations for traditional sources.

In-text citation:

W. T. Gormley, Jr., T. Gayer, D. Phillips, and B. Dawson (2005) take on the topic of pre-K programs.

In the references list, guidelines for traditional citation apply. Provide as much information as you can glean from the internet source. Note that you don't need to include the website address if the source also appears in print. Rather, just put "electronic version" in brackets after the title.

References list entry:

Dawson, B., Gayer, T., Gormley, W. T., & Phillips, D. (2005). The effects of universal pre-K on cognitive development. [Electronic version] *Developmental Psychology*, *41*, 872–884.

For sources available only online, note the date on which you found the source. Also, note the web address.

References list entry:

Feng, B. (2005). Understanding the cultural narratives of the migrant Chinese mainlanders living in Northern Ireland. *Electronic Journal of Sociology*. Retrieved December 1, 2005, from http://www.sociology.org/content/2005/tier1/feng.html

Note that APA does not use < > around the URL.

Websites with No Author Online sources that do not list an author should be identified by title.

In-text citation:

According to the Code of Federal Regulations (2005), each volume is updated once a year.

In the references list, alphabetize by the source's title.

References list entry:

Code of federal regulations. (2005). Retrieved May 14, 2005, from http://www.gpoaccess.gov/cfr/about.html

Article from Online Newspaper If you found an article on a newspaper's website, cite as a normal newspaper article in the text of your paper. In the references list, provide the general web address rather than the exact URL pointing to the article.

References list entry:

Revkin, A. (2005, Dec. 4). On climate change, a change in thinking. *New York Times.* Retrieved December 4, 2005, from http://www.nytimes.com

Online Library Resources Citation rules for such services as *EBSCO, JSTOR* and *PsycINFO* are similar to citation rules governing websites. In this example, the writer is citing an article found on EBSCO.

In-text citation:

Richard Lipkin (2005) says that the unconscious is something of an unknown quantity.

In your references list, provide as much of the following information as possible, in this order:

1. The author's name
2. The publication date
3. The material's title

4. The name(s) of the editor(s).
5. The journal's volume number
6. The page numbers
7. The date on which you accessed the source
8. The name of the source

Here is an example of a full citation from EBSCO.

References list entry:

Lipkin, R. (2005). Magic, mystery, or mechanism. *Scientific American Mind, 16* (4), 92. Retrieved November 30, 2005, from EBSCO database.

Learn APA Style: Other Rules

Familiarizing yourself with the specifics of APA style will ensure that your paper appears professional. Make sure you follow these basic guidelines.

Providing the Year Even if you're making only brief mention of a theory or experiment, provide its year in parentheses just after the author's last name.

> Because of the revolutionary theory Smith (1999) proposed, the thinking took a new direction, as we see in the work of at least two major figures (Garcia, 2000; Hoff, 2001).

Verb Tense Use the past tense ("Glendon theorized") or the present perfect tense ("Glendon has theorized") when referring to what your sources say.

> **INCORRECT:** In *Rights Talk*, Glendon **writes**, "The American property saga starts with John Locke" (1991, p. 20).
> **CORRECT:** In *Rights Talk*, Glendon **wrote**, "The American property saga starts with John Locke" (1991, p. 20).
> **CORRECT:** Glendon **has written**, "The American property saga starts with John Locke" (1991, p. 20).

Punctuation Periods go outside the closing quotation marks and the closing parenthesis for in-text citations. If you're quoting something that includes a quotation, the quotation marks in the original text turn into single quotation marks in your paper. The following sentence illustrates both rules:

> Newman (2004) writes, "[t]he ambiguity of language may also lead to catastrophe . . . Imagine that a nightguard . . . notices some gasoline drums in the corner under a sign that says 'Empty Barrels'" (p. 56).

If the original sentence ends in a question mark or an exclamation point, keep that *inside* the closing quotation mark. The citation in parentheses comes after that, with no period after it:

> He urges us to think, "What are some of the reasons people ask to see our drivers licenses?" (Newman, 2004, p. 139)

If you want to include a semicolon in the middle of a sentence, after a quotation, put the page in the following place:

Newman (2004) writes, "the doctrines of your religions may limit your behavioral choices" (p. 5); for this reason, among others, our decisions are not made freely.

Format for Long Quotations Quotations of forty words or more should be set off from the text. Indent about five spaces (half an inch, or one tab).

> Any discussion of dream interpretation must include mention of Freud. Freud writes:
>
> > I have been forced to perceive that here, once more, we have one of those not infrequent cases where an ancient and stubbornly retained popular belief seems to have come nearer to the truth of the matter than the opinion of modern science. I must insist that the dream actually does possess a meaning, and that a scientific method of dream-interpretation is possible. (*Interpretation*, 1997, p. 14)

Notice that there are no quotation marks around the quotation, and the citation at the end comes *after* the period.

Capitalization APA style says that in the references list, you must capitalize only the first word of books' titles and subtitles and capitalize periodical names normally. Note that in the body of your paper, however, you must capitalize *all* titles normally, book titles included.

Learn APA Style: Paper Format

Formatting your paper according to APA style will show your readers that you are a reliable, conscientious source of information. Here are the guidelines you need to know.

Materials

- Use standard 8½" x 11" white paper.
- Paper clip the pages (do not staple).
- No title page is necessary. APA doesn't give instructions about title pages; ask your instructor if he or she has specific requirements.

Page Numbers

- Numbers go on the upper right-hand corner of each page.
- Precede each page number with five spaces and a shortened version of your paper title.

Margins

- Use one-inch margins on all sides.
- Left-align your text—don't center it.

Spacing

- Double-space the entire paper, including the references list.
- Don't add extra space between the title and the body, or between paragraphs.
- Indent each opening sentence five spaces (one-half an inch).

Abstracts (a brief overview of your paper)

- Write and center the word *Abstract* above the text.
- The text should consist of 75 to 100 words.
- This is not necessarily required; check with your instructor.

Headings (titles of parts of your paper)

- Center headings; capitalize each word except short prepositions, coordinating conjunctions, and articles.
- These are not necessarily required; check with your instructor.

References List

- Begin the list on a new page at the end of the paper.
- Center the words *References List* above the list.
- Double-space each entry.
- Italicize book titles.
- Capitalize first words only of book and article titles; capitalize periodical names normally.

- Abbreviate *page* to *p.* and *pages* to *pp.* when referencing articles in newspapers and books; simply write the numbers when referencing journals and magazines.
- Alphabetize by authors' or editors' last names.
- List author's last name first, followed by first initial(s). Do not list first names.
- Separate multiple authors with ampersands and commas. Name the first six authors; for additional authors, omit names and add *et al.*
- If no author exists, alphabetize by title (ignore articles such as A and *The*).
- If you're listing more than one work by the same author, list the works by year of publication, beginning with the earliest date. List the author's name in each entry. Multiple works by one author within the same year should be listed alphabetically by title and identified by sequential lowercase letters.
- List the full date for articles, in the following format: (2005a, Dec. 5).
- First line should be flush left; indent next lines by five spaces (one-half inch).
- Remove hyperlinks.

Understand Other Styles

When it comes to citation, you should always follow the style your instructor requests. You might be asked to use *The Chicago Manual of Style* for your English paper, Council of Biology Editors (CBE) style for your biology paper, Linguistic Society of America (LSA) style for your linguistics paper, or American Institute of Physics (AIP) style for your physics paper. We don't have space to cover all of the possibilities, but we urge you to cite carefully according to the style appropriate for your paper. For details about each of these documentation styles, ask your instructor.

Revising Your Work

Congratulations—you've finished your first draft and gotten everything down on paper. You're heading into the final lap of the research paper marathon. But don't underestimate the hard running still left to do. Revising is not just a matter of changing a word here and deleting a comma there. While that kind of polishing is a key part of revision, it is also the last and in some ways the easiest part. Before you polish, you must tackle the big issues in your paper, such as organization and logic.

10

In her book *Bird by Bird*, writer Annie Lamott calls our first efforts "sh*tty first drafts." She says, "All good writers write them. This is how they end up with good second drafts and terrific third drafts." Even if you're an immensely skilled writer, it's almost certain that your first draft will benefit from major revisions. Brutal honesty will be one of your most useful tools, so try to see your work through your instructor's eyes.

Take a Day Off

You may have had the experience of rereading a diary entry or paper you wrote a few years ago. If you have, you know that distance can really change your perspective—and make bad writing painfully easy to spot. Getting just a little distance from your paper can help you see its errors and identify its strong points. Before you begin revising, take a day off. Don't look at or even think about your paper. The idea is to come back to your work with a fresh perspective. This will help you achieve the goal of reading through your instructor's eyes.

Start Big, End Small

When you revise, you shouldn't hack into your paper willy-nilly, changing whatever you want to in any order at all. You'll wind up doing unnecessary work, or undoing things you just did. To create a great revision efficiently, you need to approach your work logically, from the outside in—focusing on large problems first, then moving on to the smaller ones.

The Big-Stuff Stage In this stage, you'll tackle the big issues, ideally in the following order:

- Organization of the paper as a whole
- Organization of individual paragraphs
- Use of evidence
- The introduction and conclusion

You'll do lots of deleting, rewriting, cutting, and pasting. At this stage, *don't* worry about things like word choice or punctuation. Fussing over a semicolon, for example, will prove to be a waste of time if the paragraph in which that semicolon appears needs major rewriting.

The Small-Stuff Stage After you've made the major changes, you can focus on smaller problems. At this stage, you'll focus on issues such as:

- Grammar
- Sentence structure
- Tone

Keep in mind that *small* doesn't mean *unimportant*. If you neglect the big stuff, your paper will be a mass of polished sentences that don't add up to anything; if you neglect the small stuff, the organization of your ideas will be obscured by the ugliness of your sentences. Successful completion of both stages will make for a great paper.

Revise the Body First

Your introduction and conclusion are vital, but the body paragraphs are the heart and soul of your paper. The body is the longest portion of your paper, and, more important, it is where you defend your thesis using your research and where your argument comes to life. For this reason, you should revise it first.

There is another excellent reason to turn first to the body: if you do major rewriting, reorganizing, and deleting, you'll almost certainly need to revisit your introduction and conclusion to reflect these changes. How you approach your introduction and conclusion will depend on the content of the body. So revising the introduction or conclusion before the body will nearly always be a waste of time.

Reorganize Paragraphs

The first step in revising the body of your paper is improving the organization of paragraphs. When you made your outline, you ordered your paragraphs in the way you thought was most logical. It's possible that your original outline worked perfectly as you wrote your first draft. But it's also possible that you changed your mind and saw new connections during the writing process. Take a look at the way you've arranged your paragraphs and ask yourself these questions:

- Does each paragraph lead logically to the next?
- Will my reader be able to follow the thread of my argument from paragraph to paragraph?
- Does each paragraph seem to be exactly where it should be?
- Does my original organizing principle work? If I chose a chronological order, does that still seem to be the best choice?

If the answer to any of these questions is *no*, you should reorganize to fix the problem.

Revision in Action: Reorganizing Paragraphs Take a look at this paragraph from the body of our first draft:

> In Annie Hall, Woody Allen turns this conventional wisdom on its head, arguing that psychoanalysis is immensely useful for women—and practically useless for men. Allen

> biographer Eric Lax writes, "Despite [Woody Allen's] long commitment to the analytic process and its beneficial aspects, his view of it is ultimately pessimistic" (79). This pessimistic view is borne out by Allen's character, who is neurotic when the film begins and a wreck when it ends. At dinner with Annie's family, Alvy characterizes his experiences in analysis as ridiculous and infantilizing, saying, "I'm making excellent progress. Pretty soon when I lie down on his couch, I won't have to wear the lobster bib" (Annie Hall). When Alvy meets Annie, he has been seeing a psychoanalyst for fifteen years, a number that gets repeated throughout the film. Annie expresses shock at this long stint in therapy, and Alvy says, jokingly, that he's close to giving up on rationality and trying for miracles: "Yeah, I'm going to give [my analyst] one more year and then I'm going to Lourdes" (Annie Hall).

In the first draft, we put this paragraph, concerning Woody Allen's negative experiences with analysis, right after the paragraph about feminist objections to Freud. This placement seems like a logical misstep. The paper focuses on Annie Hall's experiences in analysis, using Alvy Singer's experiences mainly as contrast. Therefore, it is confusing to the reader if the first paragraph of film analysis focuses on Woody Allen and his filmic alter ego, rather than on Annie Hall.

Identifying this problem makes us think about a major organizational issue with our first draft: the discussion of Annie and Alvy does not unfold in a clear, organized manner. Paragraph C is all about Alvy, paragraph D is all about Annie, and paragraphs E and F are about Annie *and* Alvy.

As we just figured out, we want our focus to be on Annie, with Alvy analyzed for *contrast*. Therefore, the most logical fix is to do a back-and-forth comparison of Annie's and Alvy's experiences, with the body paragraph A devoted to Annie, B to Alvy, C to Annie, and so on. So in our revision, the paragraph above comes *after* our discussion of the change in Annie's speech:

> Annie is a self-loathing girl when she embarks on her relationship with Alvy, and an independent woman when it ends—all thanks to analysis. When she first meets Alvy, Annie can hardly form a complete sentence without savagely mocking herself. After Alvy contemplates her tennis skills, saying she plays well, Annie responds,
>
> > Oh, yeah? So do you. Oh, God, what a—what a dumb thing to say, right? I mean, you say it, "You play well," and right away, I have to say you play well. Oh, oh . . . God, Annie. Well . . . oh, well . . . lad-di-da, la-di-da, la-la.
>
> At the end of this agonizing speech, Annie comes close to linguistic breakdown, abandoning adult English for nonsense songs. When she invites Alvy to her apartment, she spends most of the visit babbling nervously and wondering if she's too dumb to date him. In many scenes, she allows Alvy to mock her for her quaint, girlish "Chippewa Falls expressions," which he finds first endearing and then annoying. Because of analysis, Annie's voice changes from weak, stuttering, and meandering to strong, precise, and cutting. Instead of enduring Alvy's mockery, Annie is able

to match wits with him. When he uses a Freudian term in his defense, saying, "I've got to see a picture exactly from the start to the finish, 'cause . . . 'cause I'm anal," Annie fires back with the assuredness of someone who has mastered the concepts: "Ha, that's a polite word for what you are." Waiting in line for a movie, Annie again relies on the vocabulary of analysis to express herself, telling Alvy, "You know, you're so egocentric that if I miss my therapy, you can only think of it in terms of how it affects you!" These pointed, quick-witted remarks contrast strikingly with the nervous, fumbling speech that Annie uses before entering analysis.

This is a fairly major structural change, but it's really going to improve the logical flow of our paper. It's important to do whatever you have to do in order to make your paper as readable and clear as possible, even if it involves significant reorganization and rewriting.

Check Setups and Payoffs

Anton Chekhov said, "If you say in the first chapter that there is a rifle hanging on the wall, in the second or third chapter it absolutely must go off." A setup is like Chekhov's rifle—a detail placed early in your paper that helps explain something (the payoff) that comes later. When you're doing major reorganizing, it's easy to get your setups and payoffs backward. For example, a sentence beginning "Smith says . . ." might accidentally get placed two paragraphs *before* a sentence beginning "Juan Smith, professor of criminal law, writes . . ." Your readers won't get the crucial information about who Smith is and why they should trust him until after they've already seen his name and read a quotation attributed to him.

Other kinds of confusion are also possible. In the process of reorganizing, you might delete an entire paragraph about the flight patterns of bluebirds, but neglect to delete the phrase "we will also examine their flight patterns" from your introductory paragraph's road map. Your readers will be distracted and confused by the absence of the promised supporting paragraph.

To avoid these kinds of blunders, it's important to verify that your setups and payoffs are in the right places as you revise. Check to see if you've moved or deleted any crucial information. If you have, revise the rest of your paper to reflect the change.

Improve Topic Sentences

Think of each paragraph in the body of your paper as a mini-paper. It must present the reader with an argument and then back up that argument. Just as you began writing your paper by thinking about the thesis, you should begin revising each supporting paragraph by thinking about its **topic sentence**.

Weak topic sentences usually indicate trouble ahead. If you weren't quite sure what you wanted to argue in the paragraph, if you were trying to squeeze two points in, or if the paragraph's argument was unsound, the problem will show up first in the topic sentence. Make sure each of your topic sentences does the following three things:

1. Reveals the point of the paragraph to come
2. Is clear and precisely worded rather than vague and abstract
3. Transitions from the preceding paragraph

Revision in Action: Improving Topic Sentences Take a look at this topic sentence from the first draft of our paper:

> Annie explores her own past and psyche.

This sentence is a weak beginning to the paragraph. It's vague, it doesn't connect to the paragraph that precedes it, and it gives readers no sense of what point this paragraph will prove. We revised it as follows:

> Annie analyzes her own feelings and alters her behavior in ways that illustrate the very definition of successful psychoanalysis.

This revised topic sentence works because it's specific and it tells readers exactly what the paragraph will argue.

Strengthen Paragraph Content

After you've perfected the topic sentences of your paragraphs, you should consider the content of the paragraphs themselves. Each sentence must connect logically to the next, and each piece of evidence must be relevant and put in context. (More on evidence in a moment.) Meandering, digressing without warning, or leaping from idea to idea without connecting those ideas for your readers will weaken your paper. During the revision process, put each of your body paragraphs to the test. Stellar paragraphs should meet the following criteria:

- One—and only one—argument is clearly presented.
- Each sentence is pulling its weight and is vital to the paragraph.
- No sentences are space-fillers.
- Ideas are presented in the most logical order possible.
- Each idea is logically and explicitly connected to the next.

Revision in Action: Strenthening Paragraph Content

Let's take a look at one of the most crucial paragraphs in the body of our paper, the one about feminist views of Freud. A clear examination of Freud's feminist views is vital to the paper, since we're writing about how psychoanalysis—a creation of Freud's—affects a female character. If this paragraph isn't a home run, the thesis of the paper is in jeopardy. In our first draft, the paragraph looks like this:

Many modern scholars agree with their 1970s' counterparts that Freud's theories are quite sexist. Nancy Chodorow, professor of Sociology at the University of California, Berkeley, and certified psychoanalyst, writes the following:

> Psychoanalysis seems often to argue sexist and even misogynist views of women's lives . . . that women must stay at home full-time with their children during these children's early years or risk serious consequences, that women are naturally passive, that career achievement is a substitute for or expression of unresolved penis envy, and so forth. (201)

In 1970s' New York, feminists characterized Freud's theories as outrageously misogynist. Psychoanalyst and clinical professor Muriel Dimen writes, "In and around 1970 . . . women were very, very angry" (208). 1970s' feminists viewed Freud's followers as soldiers in the war against gender equality. According to Dimen, "The feminism of that time saw in the psychoanalytic construction of the female body the pernicious machinery of patriarchal power" (208).

Remember that this is a draft—there are some errors in this paragraph that we'll fix later on. For now, we'll focus on content, which is not arranged in the most logical way possible. As a general rule, it's almost always best to tackle events chronologically, rather than jumbling them out of order. *Annie Hall* is a film made and set in the 1970s, so discussing modern-day ideas before getting to the seventies isn't appropriate. We revised the paragraph accordingly:

In 1970s' New York, feminists objected to Freud's theories, which they characterized as misogynist. Psychoanalyst and clinical professor Muriel Dimen writes, "In and around 1970 . . . women were very, very angry" (208). 1970s feminists viewed Freud's followers as soldiers in the war against gender equality. According to Dimen, "The feminism of that time saw in the psychoanalytic construction of the female body the pernicious machinery of patriarchal power" (208). It is difficult to dismiss these objections as the shrill paranoia of bra-burners, since most modern scholars of psychology agree with these 1970s' criticisms. Nancy Chodorow, professor of Sociology at the University of California, Berkeley, and certified psychoanalyst, writes the following:

> Psychoanalysis seems often to argue sexist and even misogynist views of women's lives . . . that women must stay at home full-time with their children during these children's early years or risk serious consequences, that women are naturally passive, that career achievement is a substitute for or expression of unresolved penis envy, and so forth. (201)

In this passage, Chodorow sets out feminists' main objections to Freud's theories of psychoanalysis, which they view as hostile toward women's professional and personal lives.

The revised paragraph addresses the criticisms in chronological order. It also adds the sentence beginning, "It is difficult to dismiss . . . ," which makes a needed link between past and present views of Freud.

Reexamine Evidence

After you've dealt with the logical flow of each paragraph, take a look at the quotations and paraphrases you've included. When you revise, you should scrutinize each one and determine whether it is working effectively enough in your paper.

You'll do one of four things to each piece of evidence:

- Remove
- Move
- Edit
- Keep

Remove Make sure you truly need each and every reference to research. Remember: long strings of quotations and uninterrupted lists of other scholars' arguments will bore your reader. Each reference you include should be absolutely necessary. Take a look at this sentence from our first draft:

> **ORIGINAL:** In her very first session, she discusses her family, her "feelings towards men," and her guilt about her "impulses toward marriage . . . and children."

The quoted material here isn't particularly interesting. There's no reason to quote rather than paraphrase. Remember: you should have a reason for quoting rather than paraphrasing. We can revise this sentence accordingly:

> **REVISED:** In her first session, she discusses her family, her relationships, and her guilt about wanting to get married and have children.

Move Sometimes appropriate citations can be made more effective if they are moved to a different place in the paragraph. Ensure that each citation is placed where it belongs logically.

> **ORIGINAL:** At dinner with Annie's family, Alvy characterizes his experiences in analysis as ridiculous and infantilizing, saying, "I'm making excellent progress. Pretty soon when I lie down on his couch, I won't have to wear the lobster bib" (Annie Hall). When Alvy meets Annie, he has been seeing a psychoanalyst for fifteen years, a number that gets repeated throughout the film. Annie expresses shock at this long stint in therapy, and Alvy says, jokingly, that he's close to giving up on rationality and trying for miracles: "Yeah, I'm going to give [my analyst] one more year and then I'm going to Lourdes" (Annie Hall).

Both of these quotations are amusing and revealing, but they're not placed in the most logical order possible. We found the lobster bib quotation hilarious, so it was the first one that came to mind when we were trying to think of evidence. As we revise, though, it's clear that the quotation that comes first in the film should be the first one we discuss. Therefore, it makes sense to reverse the order of the quotations.

> **REVISED:** When Alvy meets Annie, he has been seeing a psychoanalyst for fifteen years, a number that gets repeated throughout the film. Annie expresses shock at this long stint in therapy, and Alvy says, jokingly, that he's close to giving up on rationality and trying for miracles: "Yeah, I'm going to give [my analyst] one more year and then I'm going to Lourdes" (Annie Hall). At dinner with Annie's family, Alvy characterizes his experiences in analysis as ridiculous and infantilizing, saying, "I'm making excellent progress. Pretty soon when I lie down on his couch, I won't have to wear the lobster bib" (Annie Hall).

Edit Occasionally a citation will be either too long or too short. Be careful to include enough of the citation to make it useful and clear, but not so much that it threatens to overwhelm your own ideas.

> **ORIGINAL:** I don't know . . . I mean, six months ago, I would have done it. I would have done it, just to please him. . . . But the thing is–I mean, since our discussions here, I feel I have a right to my own feelings. I think you would've been happy, because . . . I really asserted myself.

This is a block quotation from a paragraph about the progress Annie makes in therapy. We've already done some editing, as the ellipses indicate, but there's more to do. The first few sentences of the quotation can be tightened up considerably with no loss of meaning. The changes we can make are small, but they increase the readability of the quotation.

> **REVISED:** [S]ix months ago, I would have done it . . . just to please him. . . . But the thing is–I mean, since our discussions here, I feel I have a right to my own feelings. I think you would've been happy, because . . . I really asserted myself.

Keep Don't feel that you must alter your citations simply because you're at the revision stage. Some or most of them will be well chosen and perfectly acceptable. And be on the lookout for places where you need *more*, not less, evidence. Do your paragraphs make any unsupported claims that would cause readers to raise their eyebrows skeptically, or think, *Says who?* Are there any places where your readers would wonder, *Okay, but what about this point that the writer isn't addressing?* If you can identify any such weak spots, you should return to your note cards and figure out how you can shore up your arguments with more evidence. In some cases, the revision process will raise new questions, and you'll have to do some additional research. This is all a normal part of the revision process.

Revise the Introduction

The job of revising the introduction will be slightly easier now that you've finished the body revisions and the arguments of your paper are fresh in your mind. Your revisions to the body paragraphs might make it necessary to change the angle, scope, or organization of the introduction; they might even make it necessary to refine your thesis. In revising your introductory paragraph, keep the following issues in mind:

- **Scope.** Are the first few sentences of your introduction too broad or too narrow? The introduction should begin with a focus slightly wider than your thesis, but it should not be so wide that you have trouble *connecting* it to your thesis.

- **Thesis Presentation.** Remember our triangle metaphor. The introduction should narrow down naturally to the point: your thesis. Make sure that the thesis strikes the reader as a unique yet natural conclusion to your introductory comments, not as a tacked-on statement.

- **Background.** The introduction should give your readers any essential background they'll need in order to understand your paper and the importance of your thesis.

- **Interest.** If your first paragraph is wordy, unfocused, or disorganized, your readers will have to force themselves to keep reading. They'll be impatient before they've even reached your thesis. Strive for a lively, interesting introductory paragraph.

- **Road Map.** Your readers will thank you if you include a brief road map of the paper somewhere close to the thesis. This way they'll know what they're about to read and get a preview of how you'll support your thesis.

Revision in Action: Revising the Introduction

Take a look at the original introduction to our paper:

> By 1977, when Annie Hall was released, Freud and his ideas were firmly entrenched in Manhattan's cultural imagination. As ?? Associate Professor of Psychoanalytic Studies at Australia's Deakin University writes, "psychoanalysis permeated American intellectual life, especially in New York." But not all privileged Manhattanites embraced Freud; feminists objected to him and his theories in the strongest terms. In his film Annie Hall, Woody Allen shows that it is in fact women who benefit most from Freud's work–specifically, Freud's theories of psychoanalysis.

There are several aspects of this introduction that cry out for attention. First, it's really boring. Some readers will be dozing off after that first sentence. The last two sentences are choppy, and the thesis (underlined) doesn't seem to flow naturally from what preceded it. No road map is provided, so readers don't know what to expect. Finally, the thesis needs some polishing. Here is our revision:

> In one of the earliest scenes in Annie Hall, a very young girl proclaims, "For God's sake, Alvy! Even Freud speaks of a latency period" (Annie Hall). The joke depends on psychoanalytic jargon, but it likely had New York audiences rolling in the aisles. By 1977, when Annie Hall was released, Freud and his ideas were firmly entrenched in Manhattan's cultural imagination. As Douglas Kirsner, Associate Professor of Psychoanalytic Studies, writes,

"psychoanalysis permeated American intellectual life, especially in New York" (Unfree Associations: Inside Psychoanalytic Institutes). But while Freud and his ideas were widely known, they were not universally admired; feminists objected to him and his theories in the strongest terms. In Annie Hall, Woody Allen takes on the widespread belief that Freud's theories were sexist. By contrasting Annie Hall's success in analysis with Alvy Singer's utter failure, he makes the case that it is women who benefit most from Freud's theories of psychoanalysis.

This introduction opens with an attention-grabbing and relevant quotation from *Annie Hall.* The lines are from the film we'll be analyzing, and they work well for the paper since they revolve around Freud and the idea of the latency period. Later in the paragraph, the phrase beginning, "while Freud and his ideas . . ." solves the problem of choppiness and links the idea of the popularity of psychoanalysis to the question of the reputation of psychoanalysis among feminists. We've added a small but effective road map: "By contrasting Annie Hall's success in analysis with Alvy Singer's utter failure . . ." This addition alerts the reader that the paper will prove its thesis by exploring this contrast.

Finally, we've made two slight but important changes to the thesis, which is underlined. First, we condensed the phrase "Freud's work—specifically, Freud's theories of psychoanalysis." The introduction has already made it clear that psychoanalysis is the topic under discussion, so the further clarification is not necessary here. Second, we changed the phrase "Allen shows" to "he makes the case." "Allen shows" is simply too strong a claim. While it's very important to sound authoritative, it's equally important to make realistic assertions. Even the most fervent Woody Allen fan wouldn't try to argue that *Annie Hall* definitively and unarguably proves that women benefit most from psychoanalysis. "He makes the case" is convincing, not wishy-washy. It neither makes wild, unprovable claims nor comes across as uncertain.

Revise the Conclusion

If you've done a thorough job of revising your paper, your conclusion will need to undergo fairly major revisions in order to match up with the changes you've made. A successful conclusion briefly gathers up all of the threads of the paper and then broadens out into a larger statement about the topic. Keep the following requirements in mind as you revise your conclusion:

- **Succinctness.** The last thing your readers want is a laborious rehashing of everything they've just read. Summarize your arguments briefly and concisely.

- **Freshness.** Try your best to sum up your thesis and arguments in a new way, rather than relying on phrases you've already used.

- **Broadness.** Make every attempt to broaden the scope—but not too far—beyond the paper's previous focus in order to demonstrate the importance or relevance of your topic in a wider context.

- **Interest.** The conclusion is the last paragraph your readers will encounter. If you rush through it, doing the written equivalent of saying, "Yada yada yada," your readers will be left with a bad impression. Slow down and take the time to make your conclusion as lively as your introduction.

Revision in Action: Revising the Conclusion Our work is really cut out for us with our original conclusion:

> In Annie Hall, Allen makes the case that in contrast to what feminist critics believe, psychoanalysis is not misogynist. On the contrary, he suggests that it is of great use to women. By contrasting Annie's wonderful experience with Alvy's terrible one, he argues that analysis can transform an awkward girl into an independent woman. One critic writes, "Individuals such as Woody Allen are constantly searching for ways to get rid of intolerable feelings and, like most artists, to put them into their work." (James). Perhaps Allen has done just that in Annie Hall.

This conclusion reads like the last gasp of a stressed, sleep-deprived writer. It relies far too heavily on summary and uses phrases that have already appeared in the paper or are only slightly changed. The phrase "independent woman," for example, featured prominently in one of our topic sentences: "Annie is a self-loathing girl when she embarks on her relationship with Alvy, and an independent woman when it ends—all thanks to analysis." Our first-draft effort suffers from rushed-conclusion syndrome: no attempt has been made to connect the quotation to the rest of the paragraph. Finally, while we made some attempt to broaden out from the film to Allen's life, the attempt fails, since it's anyone's guess what that last sentence means. Here is our revised conclusion:

> Toward the end of Annie Hall, as Annie heads off for a glamorous night at the Emmys and a sullen Alvy gets sprung from jail, the psychoanalytic moral is clear: contrary to popular belief, analysis doesn't work for men, but it can transform nervous, self-loathing women into confident, self-sufficient ones. Even if analysis doesn't work for Allen's character, the very existence of the film suggests that Allen himself has found other ways of coping. According to journalist Oliver James, artists like Woody Allen want both to expunge their neuroses and to use those neuroses in their art. The inspiration for Annie Hall was Allen and Diane Keaton's real-life relationship; according to Allen biographer Marion Meade, that relationship ended in a "protracted and painful" way (109). By transforming an unhappy breakup into one of the most popular comedies in film history, perhaps Allen found some measure of the happiness that his character Annie attains with the aid of analysis.

This conclusion summarizes what's come before, but it doesn't spend too long doing it. It also generates new phrases instead of using tired old ones. In this revision, we tied Oliver James's argument to the rest of the paragraph and used it to make the point that Allen turned his neuroses into art, thus broadening the scope. Note that we quoted James in the first draft and paraphrased him this time around. James's original words aren't particularly fascinating, so there's no reason to quote them. Finally, this conclusion broadens out to encompass Allen's life and *Annie Hall's* place in film history, and it does so in a clear and intelligible way.

Pay Attention to Tone

Research papers are nearly always best served by a formal yet lively tone. You want to let your enthusiasm shine through without lapsing into informality and show due respect for your topic and for your readers without coming across as stiff or dull. As you revise, you can rely on your own opinions for guidance as you strive to find the right tone. Think about bloggers whose posts you find abrasive, newspaper columnists whose jokes are always inappropriate, textbooks whose boring prose has nearly sent you into a coma, and emailers whose veiled insults have made you grind your teeth. Your own reactions to these varying tones will be helpful in your own work. Try to emulate those writers whose tone you admire and avoid the mistakes of writers whose tone you dislike.

There are five important issues to consider when you set out to master the tone of your paper:

1. Consistency
2. Conviction
3. Point of view
4. Respect
5. Jokiness

Consistency Whatever tone you strike, be sure to stick with it throughout your paper. Your readers will be jolted if they encounter an extremely exuberant sentence right after a very neutral one. In order to maintain your status as an authority that readers can trust, you must maintain a consistent tone.

> **INCONSISTENT:** The next painting exemplifies a similar technique. Anyone who doesn't notice that might be either blind or lying.

> **CONSISTENT:** The next painting exemplifies a similar technique. This technique will likely be obvious even to the most casual observer.

Conviction It's important to write with authority. Often, students who are arguing a bold point aren't quite sure of themselves, so they water down their prose with phrases like "I feel," "it seems that," or "one could argue." This is a mistake. Your instructor knows that you are defending *opinions,* not regurgitating facts. Your job in your paper is to convince your readers to buy your argument. To do this, you must write with conviction. Even if you need to leave room for debate or if you want to avoid sounding falsely sure of something, writing with conviction is possible. Simply use phrases such as "some critics assert," "she indicates," or "he suggests." These words signal to your readers that you realize there is room for discussion on the matter. Take a look at these examples, with the key words that produce the tone italicized:

WISHY-WASHY: *I feel* that Spenser's Britomart functions mainly as a reader of symbols.

FALSELY SURE: Britomart's *only* important role is *clearly* as a reader of symbols.

AUTHORITATIVE: Britomart's reaction to the tapestries *suggests* that she is a reader of symbols.

Point of View Many students believe that it is always incorrect to use the first-person point of view (*I, me, mine,* and so on). Many instructors share this belief, and you should check with yours to find out where he or she stands. There is a clear reason for this guideline: using the first-person draws attention to you as the writer, which is often inappropriate. Research papers gather together and analyze the opinions of experts. While your analysis of those expert opinions is crucial, you should try to omit overt references to yourself. Phrases such as "I believe" and "it seems clear to me" can weaken your argument, since readers may wonder why they should listen to you. The general and imaginary "we" is sometimes more acceptable, but even this can undermine the persuasiveness of your essay.

You can almost always find a way to avoid any self-reference. Take a look at these examples:

WEAK: For another example of the importance of healthy interactions between editorial and business staff members, I will turn to a discussion of the *New York Times.*

BETTER: For another example of the importance of healthy interactions between editorial and business staff members, we will turn to a discussion of the *New York Times*.

BEST: The *New York Times* provides another example of the importance of healthy interactions between editorial and business staff members.

All three examples say the same thing, and all three are "correct," but the third example is most authoritative.

While the third-person is best for most research papers, the first-person *can* be used effectively in some cases. If you're writing about a humorous topic, for example, or linking your research to your own experience, the occasional *I* or *my* may be desirable. If you do use the first person, use it deliberately and carefully, and ensure that your instructor has no objections.

Respect You should always avoid sounding angry, disrespectful, or sarcastic in your paper. Your readers will be put off if they sense that you feel superior to your topic. Be sure to treat with respect even those sources you disagree with vehemently.

DISRESPECTFUL: Volard's comments can be easily dismissed as the ramblings of a madman who knows nothing about the subject.

RESPECTFUL: Volard's position has attracted a broad audience, but it is less convincing than that of his peer, Grageda.

Jokiness While a few glints of humor here or there can provide a welcome relief for your readers and even show off your intelligence, outright jokiness is inappropriate in a paper. It will distract your readers and give the impression that you don't take your topic seriously.

> **JOKEY:** The symbolism in this passage is painfully obvious. Can anyone say *paging Doctor Freud*?
>
> **HUMOROUS:** Allen's obsession would give Freud plenty of material for interpretation.

Hide Your Thesaurus

The very best writing is clear and straightforward. When you're revising your own prose, strive for simple, clear language rather than complex sentences full of ten-dollar words. Unusual synonyms from a thesaurus won't make your paper more sophisticated—they'll obscure your meaning, especially if you use them incorrectly. In order to make a new word your own and use it correctly in your writing, you need to read that word over and over again, in a variety of contexts, until you grasp its subtle shades of meaning and the conventions surrounding its usage. Take a look at the following passage:

> The obstreperous student insisted upon using convoluted words of the most abstruse sort, despite the adroit advice of the sage book, which she outflanked with not the slightest qualms.

There are a few key points to be made about this sort of writing:

- **It's inaccurate.** Several of the words here are technically correct but tonally off. "Adroit advice," for example, is not conventional usage. We might chalk it up to originality were it not so obvious that this writer doesn't understand the words she's using. For example, it's clear that the writer looked up the verb "ignore" in her thesaurus and found "outflank," which she then used incorrectly.

- **It won't fool your instructor.** If you throw in fancy words willy-nilly, your instructor will sense from a mile away that you're faking it. Fancy writing *does not* make you seem smarter; it simply makes you seem like a ten-year-old kid trying to look natural while wearing his father's enormous suit jacket.

- **It's beneath you.** The words you know and feel comfortable with will be absolutely sufficient if they are grammatically correct.

Use Transitions

Transitions are magic words that will make your reader feel oriented within your paper. An important part of the revision process is making sure that you've made clear transitions from paragraph to paragraph and from sentence to sentence. Transitions can do several things:

- **Show forward movement.** Words like *additionally, also,* and *furthermore* indicate that the next sentence follows from the previous one.

  EXAMPLE: Transitions help your reader follow your argument. *Additionally,* they force you to make explicit the connections between your ideas.

- **Establish cause and effect.** Words and phrases such as *therefore, so,* and *as a result* suggest that the previous idea causes the following one.

  EXAMPLE: Without transitions, your reader won't be able to make the connections. *Therefore,* it's crucial to include transitional words and phrases.

- **Demonstrate conflict.** *However, but, although,* and *in contrast* show that what you're about to argue conflicts or takes a new tack than did your previous point.

  EXAMPLE: Some students feel that their readers will intuitively grasp the connection between their arguments. *However,* these students are sadly mistaken.

Like signposts on a road, transitional words and phrases signal the direction of your argument and show your reader where you are going.

Vary Sentence Structure

In the first draft, your goal was to get everything down on paper clearly, without worrying about the elegance of your sentences. During the revision process, you should figure out how to make your paper sophisticated and pleasurable to read. Elevating your prose in this way involves varying your sentence structure. It is tedious to read sentences that are all of the same length and shape, such as in this example:

> Revision can be kind of fun. Revision gives you time to identify your mistakes. Revision gives you the chance to fix your writing. If you come across a passage like this, you can change it. In revision you can make a repetitive passage more exciting by mixing up the sentence structure.

Each sentence in this passage is very basic, and most of the sentences are of the same length and use the same kind of construction. As you can see, passages consisting of sentence upon sentence like this are agonizing to read. You can avoid torturing your readers by doing three things:

1. **Varying sentence length.** There is no perfect length for sentences; long ones can be just as effective as short or medium ones. The key is to refrain from stacking one short sentence after another, or one long sentence after another. Variation in length is the spice of your research paper.

2. **Varying sentence openings.** Beginning sentence after

sentence in exactly the same way will produce the impression of a chant or a prayer, rather than a sophisticated paper. It is unacceptable, for example, to have three sentences in a row that begin with the word "revision."

3. **Rearranging the parts of speech.** Your prose will be much more interesting if it doesn't follow a formula such as noun + verb ("Revision can be," "Revision gives"). Vary the way you arrange the parts of speech.

There are a number of ways to revise the previous passage according to these rules. Here is one possibility:

> Revision gives you time to identify and fix your mistakes. If you come across a passage full of unvaried sentences, you can change it by mixing up the structure. In fact, revision can be kind of fun.

This revision begins with a medium sentence, moves to a long sentence, and ends with a short sentence. No two sentences begin in the same way, and the parts of speech aren't plugged into a formula.

Avoid Repetition

The mind tends to get into ruts when you're writing. If you use the word *scrumptious* in your first paragraph, chances are good that *scrumptious* will be the first word that pops into your head when you're writing your fourth paragraph and need a word to describe Julia Child's creations. *So what?* you ask. *"Scrumptious" is a great word!* True, but even the best words lose their luster with overuse. Your readers long to be surprised, informed, and amused by each sentence of your paper, and the repetition of words will be annoying, even if the word is entertaining and even if its second occurrence comes ten pages after its first.

Do your level best to avoid repeating even those words that have no simile, such as *pool*. If necessary, rewrite sentences to avoid repetition:

REPETITIVE: As the kids dashed toward the pool house to change, the swimming pool glinted invitingly in the sun.
NONREPETITIVE: As the kids dashed to get changed, the swimming pool glinted invitingly in the sun.

Eliminate Passive Voice

The passive voice occurs when you use any form of the verb "to be" plus the past participle of a verb: "is eaten," "were seen." In revision, eliminate the passive voice from your writing wherever possible—it weakens your prose. The passive voice takes the emphasis away from the subject:

PASSIVE: The dog was chased by the ferocious cat.
ACTIVE: The ferocious cat chased the dog.

Getting rid of all those *is*'s and *was*'s will force you to come up with interesting verbs, which will make your writing thousands of times more exciting to read:

BORING: The robber was hidden by the shadows.

EXCITING: The robber skulked in the shadows.

You won't be able to eliminate every instance of passive voice from your writing, nor should you try. Sometimes sentences demand passive voice:

PASSIVE AND PLEASANT: The south of Spain is known for its flamenco tradition.

ACTIVE AND ODD: Visitors know the south of Spain for its flamenco tradition.

Proofread Your Work

Proofreading can be a relief after all the mental strain of writing and revising, but checking for grammar, spelling, and punctuation still requires your close attention. There are three important tips to keep in mind:

1. **Don't rely on the spelling and grammar check.** Automatic checks on your computer can be a huge help, but they can't do everything. Only you have the smarts to notice that you wrote *sea* when you meant *see*, or that the second citation in paragraph five refers to page 1,567 instead of page 156.

2. **Print it out.** For some mysterious reason, it's much easier to see mistakes when you're looking at the printed page than when you're squinting at your computer screen. You'll get the best proofreading results if you print out your work.

3. **Read out loud.** Reading your work out loud forces you to slow down and pay attention to small words that your eye might skim over, and it allows you to hear the rhythm of your sentences.

Citations One crucial part of proofreading is carefully checking your citations to make sure that each one is formatted correctly. Ensure that all of your paraphrases and quotations are properly credited according to whichever style your instructor has asked you to follow. Make sure every page number, close quotation mark, period, comma, last name, and so on are in the appropriate spot.

In our first draft, for example, many of our quotations from *Annie Hall* are formatted incorrectly.

> **INCORRECT:** Alvy contrasts Annie's success and his failure explicitly: "She's making progress and I'm not making any progress."

This is a quotation from a film, but that doesn't mean we can use any kind of format we please. The citation must adhere to MLA standards. That means we must credit the source and place the final punctuation mark outside the close quotation mark, rather than inside it.

> **CORRECT:** Alvy contrasts Annie's success and his failure explicitly, telling his analyst, "She's making progress and I'm not making any progress" (Annie Hall).

Now is also the time to check your in-text citations against your works cited or references list. Ensure that every source you mention in your text is credited in your works cited or references list as needed and that every source mentioned in your works cited or references list actually appears in your text.

Format Carefully

Now's the time to make sure you've formatted your paper according to the appropriate documentation style. See page 158 for MLA guidelines and page 175 for APA guidelines, or ask your instructor.

Presenting Your Work In one of Bill Watterson's *Calvin and Hobbes* comic strips, Calvin assures Hobbes that a total lack of effort won't affect his research paper: "I've got a secret weapon that will *guarantee* a good grade! No teacher can resist *this*! A clear plastic binder!" Fancy, expensive trappings can make your paper look nice, but they won't distract your instructor from the content of your paper (or lack thereof, as Calvin discovers). Just make sure your research paper is legible and printed on paper of reasonably high-quality stock that is free of food stains and wrinkles.

Model Research Paper in Action

Throughout this book, we've shown you bits and pieces of our writing process for our paper on Annie Hall. Along the way, we brainstormed, chose a topic, researched, created a thesis, outlined, and learned how to cite sources correctly. All of these steps are distinct, and each must be handled carefully—without a strong foundation, our research paper would not be successful.

What follows here is the actual paper we've created as we followed all the steps we laid out for you in this book. We give you both the first draft and the revision so you can see how a real paper takes shape, from the first steps to the last. And we include lots of commentary so you can see exactly how abstract concepts work in a real paper.

First Draft in Action

Below is the first draft of our research paper on *Annie Hall*. As you read it, look for the elements we've discussed:

- A brief introduction that provides readers with a context for the topic
- A thesis statement
- A transition and introduction for each supporting argument

- A body with a logical flow, interwoven reasons and examples, and relevant citations
- A conclusion that summarizes the thesis without restating it and then broadens the scope of the paper

In this draft, we've labeled each part according to the elements in our outline from Chapter 6 so you can see exactly how we've gone from outline to draft.

Brooks Emmett

First Draft

INTRODUCTION

By 1977, when Annie Hall was released, Freud and his ideas were firmly entrenched in Manhattan's cultural imagination. As ?? Associate Professor of Psychoanalytic Studies at Australia's Deakin University writes, "psych analysis permeated American intellectual life, especially in New York." But not all privileged Manhattanites embraced Freud; feminists objected to him and his theories in the strongest terms. In his film Annie Hall, Woody Allen shows that it is in fact women who benefit most from Freud's work—specifically, Freud's theories of psychoanalysis.

BODY: First major supporting argument

Many modern scholars agree with their 1970s counterparts that Freud's theories are quite sexist. Nancy Chodorow, professor of Sociology at the University of California, Berkeley, and certified psychoanalyst, writes,

> Psychoanalysis seems often to argue sexist and even misogynist views of women's lives . . . that women must stay at home

full-time with their children during these children's early years or risk serious consequences, that women are naturally passive, that career achievement is a substitute for or expression of unresolved penis envy, and so forth. (201)

In 1970s' New York, feminists characterized Freud's theories as outrageously misogynist. Psychoanalyst and clinical professor Muriel Dimen writes, "In and around 1970 . . . women were very, very angry" (208). 1970s' feminists viewed Freud's followers as soldiers in the war against gender equality. According to Dimen, "The feminism of that time saw in the psychoanalytic construction of the female body the pernicious machinery of patriarchal power" (208).

BODY: Second major supporting argument

In Annie Hall, Woody Allen turns this conditional wisdom on its head, arguing that psychoanalsis is immensely useful for women and practically useless for men. Allen biographer Eric Lax writes, "Despite [Woody Allen's] long commitment to the analytic process and its beneficial aspects, his view of it is ultimately pessimistic" (79). This pess mistic view is born out by Allen's character, who is neurotic when the film begins and a wreck when it ends. At dinner with Annie's family, Alvy characterizes his experiences in analysis as ridiculous and infantilizing, saying, "I'm making excellent progress. Pretty soon when I lie down on his couch, I won't have to wear the lobster bib" (Annie Hall). When Alvy meets Annie, he has been seeing a psychoanalyst for fifteen years, a number that gets repeated throughout the film. Annie expresses shock at this long stint in therapy, and Alvy says, jokingly, that he's close to giving up on rationality and trying for miracles: "Yeah, I'm going to give [my analyst] one more year and then I'm going to Lourdes" (Annie Hall).

BODY: Third major supporting argument

Annie is a self-loathing girl when she embarks on her relationship with Alvy, and an independent woman when it ends—all thanks to analysis. When she first meets Alvy, Annie can hardly form a complete sentence without savagely mocking herself. After Alvy contemplates her tennis skills, saying she plays well, Annie responds,

> "Oh, yeah? So do you. Oh, God, what a—what a dumb thing to say, right? I mean, you say it, 'You play well,' and right away, I have to say you play well. Oh, oh . . . God, Annie. Well . . . oh, well . . . lad-di-da, la-di-da, la-la."

At the end of this agonizing speech, Annie comes close to linguistic breakdown, abandoning adult English for nonsense songs. When she invites Alvy to her apartment, she spends most of the visit babbling nervously and wondering if she's too dumb to date him. In many scenes, she allows Alvy to mock her for her quaint, girlish "Chippewa Falls expressions," which he finds first endearing and then annoying. Because of analysis, Annie's voice changes from weak, stuttering, and meandering to strong, precise, and cutting. Instead of enduring Alvy's mockery, Annie is able to match wits with him. When he uses a Freudian term in his defense, saying, "I've got to see a picture exactly from the start to the finish ,'cause . . . 'cause I'm anal," Annie fires back with the assuredness of someone who has mastered the concepts: "Ha, that's a polite word for what you are." Waiting in line for a movie, Annie again relies on the vocabulary of analysis to express herself, telling Alvy, "You know, you're so egocentric that if I miss my therapy you can only think of it in terms of how it affects you!" These pointed, quick-witted remarks contrast strikingly with the nervous, fumbling speech that Annie uses before entering analysis.

BODY: Fourth major supporting argument

Annie explores her own past and psyche in analysis, whereas Alvy accomplishes very little. In her very first session, she discusses her family, her "feelings towards men," and her guilt about her "impulses toward marriage . . . and children." She recovers an important memory about her parents and cries. She also analyzes a dream in which she breaks Frank Sinatra's glasses. Her analyst points out that Alvy's last name is Singer, which lines up with Sinatra; Alvy wears glasses; the implication is that Annie dreams of harming Alvy. Later, in a session intercut with one of Alvy's sessions, Annie describes refusing to sleep with Alvy:

> "I don't know . . . I mean, six months ago, I would have done it. I would have done it, just to please him. . . . But the thing is—I mean, since our discussions here, I feel I have a right to my own feelings. I think you would've been happy, because . . . I really asserted myself."

Alvy's sessions are substantially less productive than Annie's. When she tells him about her first experience, he says, "All this happened in the first hour? . . . That's amazing . . . I've been going for fifteen years . . . I don't get . . . nothing like that." He points out that he has never once cried during analysis. And his attempt to pick apart Annie's dream falls flat. Eric Lax quotes a conversation Allen had with the director Robert Altman, in which Allen said, "The first time you're in psychoanalysis and dreams are interpreted for you, with you, there's a sort of exhilarating feeling that you're putting a puzzle together. But . . . I never learned a scintilla about myself from a dream." Allen's character displays an identical obtuseness, claiming that Annie's dream means she is trying to suffocate herself—a claim Annie refutes by citing her therapist. In the intercut scenes, Alvy contrasts Annie's success and his failure explicitly: "She's making progress, and I'm not making any progress."

BODY: Fifth major supporting argument

Analysis gives Annie tools she can use in the real world, whereas it gives Alvy no tools. Analysis gives Annie tools she can use in the real world. After she and Alvy split up, she draws on her therapy for support, saying, "My analyst thinks this is a key move for me." She moves to Los Angeles and begins a new relationship. When Alvy flies out to beg her to come back to him, she demurs, again relying on what she's learned in analysis: "Alvy, you're incapable of enjoying life, you know that? I mean, your life is New York City . . . You're like this island unto yourself." She has found a way to be happy, and she has gained the independence of spirit to pursue that happiness. Alvy, in contrast, has gained a great deal of theoretical understanding, but very little that is of use in the real world. Analysis does not help him weather the breakup. He carries a bar of Annie's soap around in his pocket like a talisman, calls himself "jealous like Medea," and tries to re-create with other women fun moments he shared with Annie. His desperate flight to L.A., where he proposes to Annie and is immediately rebuffed, underlines his bad mental health. Just after Annie rejects him for the last time, Alvy gets into a fender-bender. He analyzes himself as he speaks to the cop on the scene, saying, "I have a terrific problem with authority" (Annie Hall). But while analysis has helped him understand his own psyche, it has not given him any tools to use in the real world; as he speaks to the cop, he rips up his own license and winds up in jail.

CONCLUSION

In Annie Hall, Allen makes the case that in contrast to what feminist critics believe, psychoanalysis is not misogynist. On the contrary, he suggests that it is of great use to women. By contrasting Annie's wonderful experience with Alvy's terrible one, he argues that analysis can transform an awkward girl into an independent woman. One critic writes, "Individuals such as Woody Allen are constantly searching for ways to get rid of intolerable feelings and, like most artists, to put them into their work." (James). Perhaps Allen has done just that in Annie Hall.

Works Cited

Chodorow, Nancy J. Feminism and Psychoanalytic Theory. New Haven and London: Yale University Press, 1989.

Lax, Eric. Woody Allen: A Biography. New York: Vintage Books, 1992.

Meade, Marion. The Unruly Life of Woody Allen (A Biography). New York: Scribner, 2000.

Roth, Michael S., ed. Freud: Conflict and Culture: Essays on His Life, Work, and Legacy. New York: Vintage Books, 2000.

Van Herik, Judith. Freud on Femininity and Faith. Berkeley and Los Angeles: University of California Press, 1982.

Comments Let's do a quick analysis of this first draft. We've already discussed the introduction, but it's worth pointing out here that one key element is still missing: the road map. While the readers will know *what* we're planning to argue in this paper, they won't know *how* we're going to argue it. In revision, we'll have to add a sentence or two to the introduction.

Each paragraph in this first draft adheres to and fleshes out our original outline. Note that quotations are introduced with signal phrases, such as "Nancy Chodorow, professor of Sociology at the University of California" and "Allen biographer Eric Lax." There is an appropriate balance between quotations, paraphrases, and our own analysis. Some of the citations are formatted incorrectly (the block quotations, for example), and a page number is missing from a citation in paragraph D. These would be major problems in the final paper, but they aren't a big deal in the first draft.

A note about format: since our instructor has asked us to follow MLA guidelines, we have to turn in a double-spaced paper. However, we decided to write single-spaced text for our first draft, since it allows us to see more of each paragraph at one time. That's one of the beauties of the first draft—no one will see it but you. You'll have time to format everything correctly during the revision process.

It's a good idea to write a draft of your works-cited list when you write the first draft of your paper. You'll be surprised how many picky little errors you'll find if you take a day away from the list and then return to it with fresh eyes. The important thing right now is that all of our information is included. We'll worry about perfecting it when we revise.

Revision in Action

A thorough revision has made our paper much stronger. Take a look at this final version. We'll explain the changes we made afterward. Remember: we're following MLA guidelines.

Brook Emmett
Professor Reel
Modern American Films
January 1, 2006

"Excellent Progress": The Unconventional Success of Analysis in Annie Hall

In one of the earliest scenes in Annie Hall, a very young girl proclaims, "For God's sake, Alvy! Even Freud speaks of a latency period." The joke depends on psychoanalytic jargon, but it likely had New York audiences rolling in the aisles. By 1977, when Annie Hall was released, Freud and his ideas were firmly entrenched in Manhattan's cultural imagination. * Douglas Kirsner, an associate professor of psychoanalytic studies at Deakin University, writes that "psychoanalysis permeated American intellectual life, especially in New York." But while Freud and his ideas

The original signal phrase was *"As ?? . . . writes."* We've replaced the question marks with the source's name.

were widely known, they were not universally admired; feminists objected to him and his theories in the strongest terms. In Annie Hall, Woody Allen challenges the widespread belief that Freud's theories were sexist. By contrasting Annie Hall's success in analysis with Alvy Singer's utter failure, he makes the case that it is women who benefit most from Freud's theories of psychoanalysis.

This phrase is our road map. It's now clear that we'll prove our thesis by going back and forth between Annie and Alvy.

In 1970s' New York, feminists rejected Freud's theories, which they characterized as misogynist. Psychoanalyst and clinical professor Muriel Dimen writes, "In and around 1970 . . . women were very, very angry" (208). Feminists in the 1970s viewed Freud's followers as soldiers in the war against gender equality. According to Dimen, "The feminism of that time saw in the psychoanalytic construction of the female body the pernicious machinery of patriarchal power" (208). It is difficult

It's awkward and incorrect to begin a sentence with numerals ("1970s feminists..."), so we rewrote the

This phrase acknowledges a possible objection–the idea that these criticisms might be the dated arguments of old-school feminists–and prepares readers for a refutation of that idea, which we get in the next sentence with Chodorow's to dismiss these objections as the shrill paranoia of bra-burners, since most modern scholars of psychology agree with these 1970s' criticisms. Nancy Chodorow, professor of sociology at the University of California, Berkeley, and certified psychoanalyst, writes:

> Psychoanalysis seems often to argue sexist and even misogynist views of women's lives . . . that women must stay at home full-time with their children during these children's early years or risk serious consequences, that women are naturally passive, that career achievement is a substitute for or expression of unresolved penis envy, and so forth. (201)

The entire block quote should be indented by five spaces, and there is no extra space between the block quote and the paragraph.

In this passage, Chodorow sets out feminists' main objections to Freud and his attitude toward women's professional and personal lives. Even self-defined defenders of Freud and his continued relevance concede the point made

In the first draft, the sentence immediately following Chodorow's quotation was this: *In 1970s New York, feminists characterized Freud's theories as outrageously misogynist.* This sentence was weak because it moved away from the quotation without doing any analysis. This new sentence spends time analyzing the quotation.

by seventies'-era feminists. Peter Kramer, clinical professor of psychiatry at Brown University, argues, "From the modern standpoint, Freud is often simply wrong . . . we disagree with almost everything he had to say about sex and gender at any stage in his career" (202).

In the first draft, this sentence was immediately followed by a discussion of Annie and Alvy's failures in analysis. It makes more sense to begin with a discussion of Annie, since she is the real focus of the paper.

*

In Annie Hall, Woody Allen turns this conventional wisdom on its head, arguing that psychoanalysis is immensely useful for women—and practically useless for men. Annie is a self-loathing girl when she embarks on her relationship with Alvy, and an independent woman when she leaves the relationship—all thanks to analysis. When she first meets Alvy, Annie can hardly form a complete sentence without savagely mocking herself. After Alvy contemplates her tennis skills, saying she plays well, Annie responds:

Oh, yeah? So do you. Oh, God, what a—what a dumb thing to say, right? I mean, you say it, 'You play well,' and right away, I have to say you play well. Oh, oh . . . God, Annie. Well . . . oh, well . . . lad-di-da, la-di-da, la-la. (Annie Hall)

Here, as in many spots of the first draft, we neglected to cite the film. It is always better to be explicit.

At the end of this agonizing speech, Annie comes close to a linguistic breakdown, abandoning adult English for nonsense songs. When she invites Alvy to her apartment, she spends most of the visit babbling nervously and wondering if she's too dumb to date him. In many scenes, she allows Alvy to mock her for her quaint, girlish "Chippewa Falls expressions", which he finds first endearing and then annoying (Annie Hall).

This paragraph had been part of the one above it. By splitting the paragraphs in two, we avoid the problem of a gigantic paragraph and give ourselves more room to work with each idea.

By showing us how Annie transforms from bashful stutterer to assured deliverer of Freudian one-liners, Allen argues that psychoanalysis is a powerful agent of change for women. He contradicts the kind of arguments

This sentence restates Allen's purpose in showing Annie's transformation.

made by critics like Madelon Sprengnether, English professor at the University of Minnesota, who believes that "psychoanalysis offers a means of comprehending the unconscious structure of patriarchy. What is does not provide is a strategy for change" (8). Because of analysis, Annie's voice changes from weak, unsure, and meandering to strong, precise, and cutting. Instead of enduring Alvy's mockery, Annie is able to match wits with him. When he uses a Freudian term in his defense, saying, "I've got to see a picture exactly from the start to the finish ,'cause . . . 'cause I'm anal," Annie fires back with the assuredness of someone who has mastered the concepts: "Ha, that's a polite word for what you are" (Annie Hall). Waiting in line for a movie, Annie again relies on the vocabulary of analysis to express herself, telling Alvy, "You know, you're so egocentric that if I miss my therapy, you can only think of

This quotation was not cited in our first draft. Its addition strengthens our paper by showing the kind of conventional wisdom that Allen is arguing against.

it in terms of how it affects you!" (Annie Hall). These pointed, quick-witted remarks contrast strikingly with the nervous, fumbling speech that Annie uses before entering analysis.

This paragraph was the second body paragraph of our first draft. Because we moved it, we needed a new topic sentence. This one transitions from our discussion of Annie with the phrase "if drastic and positive change characterize Annie's therapeutic experience" and then makes the point we will argue clear: "frustrating stasis characterizes Alvy's."

If drastic and positive change characterizes Annie's therapeu- * tic experience, frustrating stasis characterizes Alvy's. Allen biographer Eric Lax writes, "Despite [Woody Allen's] long commitment to the analytic process and its beneficial aspects, his view of it is ultimately pessimistic" (79). This pessimistic view is born out by Allen's character, who is neurotic when his relationship with Annie begins and a wreck when it ends. When Alvy meets Annie, he has been seeing a psychoanalyst for fifteen years, a number that gets repeated throughout the film. Annie expresses shock at this long stint in therapy, and Alvy says, jokingly, that he's close to giving up on rationality and trying for miracles: "Yeah, I'm going to give [my analyst] one more year and then I'm going to Lourdes" (Annie Hall). At dinner with Annie's family, Alvy characterizes his experiences in analysis as ridiculous and infantilizing, saying, "I'm making excellent progress. Pretty soon when I lie down on his couch, I won't have to wear the lobster bib" (Annie Hall).

Annie analyzes her own feelings and alters her behavior * in ways that illustrate the very definition of successful psychoanalysis. In her first session, she discusses her family, her relationships, and her guilt about wanting to get married and have children. She recovers an important memory about her parents and cries. She also analyzes a dream in which she breaks Frank Sinatra's glasses. Her analyst points out that Alvy's last name is Singer, which lines up with Sinatra; Alvy wears glasses; the implication is that Annie dreams of harming Alvy.

Our original topic sentence read as follows: *Annie explores her own past and psyche in analysis, whereas Alvy accomplishes very little.* That sentence is vague and dull; and in our new structure, this paragraph deals with Annie exclusively. Our revised topic sentence is more specific and analytical, and it prepares the reader for the point that will be argued in the next paragraph.

Later, in a session intercut with one of Alvy's sessions, Annie describes refusing to sleep with Alvy:

> "[S]ix months ago, I would have done it . . . just to please him. . . . But the thing is—I mean, since our discussions here, I feel I have a right to my own feelings. I think you would've been happy, because . . . I really asserted myself." (Annie Hall)

In these lines, Annie credits analysis with making her believe that she has "a right to [her] own feelings," and giving her the ability to assert herself. Her steady emotional progress is a textbook success.

In our first draft, we raced away from the quotation without analyzing it. This is a common problem in first drafts, when the impulse is to get the right quotation into the text and then move on. Here we slow down and do strong interpretive work of Annie's musings.

Alvy's sessions are substantially less productive than Annie's. When she tells him about her first experience, he says, "All this happened in the first hour? . . . That's amazing . . . I've been going for fifteen years . . . I don't get . . . nothing like that." He points out that he has never once cried during analysis. And his attempt to pick apart Annie's dream falls flat. Lax quotes a conversation Allen had with the director Robert Altman, in which Allen said, "The first time you're in psychoanalysis and dreams are interpreted for you, with you, there's a sort of exhilarating feeling that you're putting a puzzle together. But . . . I never learned a scintilla about myself from a dream" (268). Allen's character displays an identical obtuseness, arguing that Annie's dream means she is trying to suffocate herself—a claim Annie refutes by citing her therapist. In the intercut scenes, Alvy contrasts Annie's success and his failure explicitly, telling his analyst, "She's making progress, and I'm not making any progress" (Annie Hall).

This page number was missing from our first draft.

We've removed two paragraphs from the first draft (the ones beginning *Analysis gives Annie tools . . . and Alvy, in contrast . . .*). We were over the required word count, and these paragraphs were the weakest ones in the paper. Cutting them was a little painful, but the paper is stronger now, and we're meeting our instructor's word limit.

Toward the end of Annie Hall, as Annie heads off for a glamorous night at the Emmys, and a sullen Alvy gets sprung from jail, the psychoanalytic moral is clear: contrary to popular belief, analysis doesn't work for men, but it can transform nervous, self-loathing women into confident, self-sufficient ones. Even if analysis doesn't work for Allen's character, the very existence of the film suggests that some version of analysis works for Allen himself. According to journalist and clinical psychologist Oliver James, artists like Woody Allen want both to expunge their neuroses and to use those neuroses in their art. The inspiration for Annie Hall was Allen and Diane Keaton's real-life relationship; according to Allen biographer Marion Meade, that relationship ended in a "protracted and painful" way (109). By transforming an unhappy breakup into one of the most popular comedies in film history, perhaps Allen found some measure of the happiness that his character Annie attains with the aid of analysis.

* We found James's article online in a UK newspaper's website. We assumed he was a journalist, but further research revealed that he is also a clinical psychologist—which makes his commentary more convincing. It's also more accurate to note his dual profession.

Works Cited

Annie Hall. Dir. Woody Allen. Perf. Woody Allen and Diane Keaton. 1977. DVD. MGM Home Entertainment, 2000.

Chodorow, Nancy J. Feminism and Psychoanalytic Theory. New Haven and London: Yale University Press, 1989.

Dimen, Muriel. "Strange Hearts: On the Paradoxical Liaison Between Psychoanalysis and Feminism." Roth 207–220.

James, Oliver. "Be a Freud … Be Very Much a Freud." The Times Online. 8 Jul. 2005. 19 Dec. 2005. <http://www.timesonline.co.uk/article/0,,7-1684529,00.html>

Kirsner, Douglas. "Unfree Associations: Inside Psychoanalytic Institutes." Human Nature Review. 1998. 21 Dec. 2005. <http://human-nature.com/kirsner/>

Kramer, Peter D. "Freud: Current Projections." Roth 196–206.

Annie Hall was a crucial omission from our first works cited list. When citing films, place the title first, followed by the director, the lead actors, the year of original release, the format, the distributor's name, and the year of your copy's release.

In the first draft, this entry and the one for Kramer, Peter D., did not exist. We cited only the anthology in which these chapters appear (see the Roth Michael S. entry). Readers would have been perplexed if they tried to look up our in-text references to Dimen and Kramer, since only the editor's name appeared in our works cited list. In the revision, we've cross-referenced Dimen's and Kramer's chapters with the anthology edited by Roth, according to MLA style.

The biggest problem with the first draft of our works cited list: we didn't include any of our online sources. This would be a horrifying mistake to make in the final paper. It happened because we simply went through the stack of books sitting on our desk rather than going through our paper thoroughly and making sure we had credited every source we cited.

Lax, Eric. Woody Allen: A Biography. New York: Vintage Books, 1992.

Meade, Marion. The Unruly Life of Woody Allen (A Biography). New York: Scribner, 2000.

Roth, Michael S., ed. Freud: Conflict and Culture: Essays on His Life, Work, and Legacy. New York: Vintage Books, 2000.

Sprengnether, Madelon. The Spectral Mother: Freud, Feminism, and Psychoanalysis. Ithaca and London: Cornell University Press, 1990.

Van Herik, Judith. Freud on Femininity and Faith. Berkeley and Los Angeles: University of California Press, 1982.

We neglected to cite Sprengnether in our first draft. When we proofread, we noticed that we had added an in-text citation and had not yet added a corresponding entry.

A Final Note

Congratulations! You've done it. Think back to all the work you've completed over the past few months or weeks. Think of the books you've read, the websites you've investigated, the searches you've conducted, the note cards you've arranged, the words you've typed, the paragraphs you've edited, the works you've cited, the extra-shot lattes you've consumed. Your accomplishment is something to be proud of.

Writing a research paper probably isn't something you'd do for fun, but the process has actually given you some valuable skills that will help you as you continue your education and your life. Believe it or not, knowing how to research a topic and utilize that research correctly will help you in the real world. Whether you're doing research into the best hybrid car on the market, writing an article for a magazine, or putting together your Ph.D. thesis, you will rely on the very tools you have just used to create a successful research paper. We hope we've helped you along the way!

About the Author

Emma Chastain grew up in Massachusetts. She graduated summa cum laude, Phi Beta Kappa from Barnard College, where she majored in English with a concentration in creative writing. She is currently working toward her master's degree in fiction at Boston University. Emma has written several articles for the New Republic's website and is the author of SparkNotes *Ultimate Style: The Rules of Writing.*